Primary Education in Malawi

A WORLD BANK STUDY

Primary Education in Malawi
Expenditures, Service Delivery, and Outcomes

Vaikalathur Ravishankar, Safaa El-Tayeb El-Kogali, Deepa Sankar,
Nobuyuki Tanaka, and Nelly Rakoto-Tiana

© 2016 International Bank for Reconstruction and Development / The World Bank
1818 H Street NW, Washington, DC 20433
Telephone: 202-473-1000; Internet: www.worldbank.org

Some rights reserved

1 2 3 4 19 18 17 16

World Bank Studies are published to communicate the results of the Bank's work to the development community with the least possible delay. The manuscript of this paper therefore has not been prepared in accordance with the procedures appropriate to formally edited texts.

This work is a product of the staff of The World Bank with external contributions. The findings, interpretations, and conclusions expressed in this work do not necessarily reflect the views of The World Bank, its Board of Executive Directors, or the governments they represent. The World Bank does not guarantee the accuracy of the data included in this work. The boundaries, colors, denominations, and other information shown on any map in this work do not imply any judgment on the part of The World Bank concerning the legal status of any territory or the endorsement or acceptance of such boundaries.

Nothing herein shall constitute or be considered to be a limitation upon or waiver of the privileges and immunities of The World Bank, all of which are specifically reserved.

Rights and Permissions

This work is available under the Creative Commons Attribution 3.0 IGO license (CC BY 3.0 IGO) http://creativecommons.org/licenses/by/3.0/igo. Under the Creative Commons Attribution license, you are free to copy, distribute, transmit, and adapt this work, including for commercial purposes, under the following conditions:

Attribution—Ravishankar, Vaikalathur, Safaa El-Tayeb El-Kogali, Deepa Sankar, Nobuyuki Tanaka, and Nelly Rakoto-Tiana. 2016. *Primary Education in Malawi: Expenditures, Service Delivery, and Outcomes.* World Bank Studies. Washington, DC: World Bank. doi: 10.1596/978-1-4648-0794-7. License: Creative Commons Attribution CC BT 3.0 IGO.

Translations—If you create a translation of this work, please add the following disclaimer along with the attribution: *This translation was not created by The World Bank and should not be considered an official World Bank translation. The World Bank shall not be liable for any content or error in this translation.*

Adaptations—If you create an adaptation of this work, please add the following disclaimer along with the attribution: *This is an adaptation of an original work by The World Bank. Views and opinions expressed in the adaptation are the sole responsibility of the author or authors of the adaptation and are not endorsed by The World Bank.*

Third-party content—The World Bank does not necessarily own each component of the content contained within the work. The World Bank therefore does not warrant that the use of any third-party-owned individual component or part contained in the work will not infringe on the rights of those third parties. The risk of claims resulting from such infringement rests solely with you. If you wish to re-use a component of the work, it is your responsibility to determine whether permission is needed for that re-use and to obtain permission from the copyright owner. Examples of components can include, but are not limited to, tables, figures, or images.

All queries on rights and licenses should be addressed to the Publishing and Knowledge Division, The World Bank, 1818 H Street NW, Washington, DC 20433, USA; fax: 202-522-2625; e-mail: pubrights@worldbank.org.

ISBN (paper): 978-1-4648-0794-7
ISBN (electronic): 978-1-4648-0799-2
DOI: 10.1596/978-1-4648-0794-7

Library of Congress Cataloging-in-Publication Data has been requested

Contents

Acknowledgments ix
About the Authors xi
Executive Summary xiii
Abbreviations xxv

Chapter 1	**Introduction**	**1**
	Context	1
	Objective and Scope	5
	Data Sources, Methodology, and Limitations	6
	Report Structure	7
	Notes	8
Chapter 2	**Expenditures and Inputs**	**9**
	Sources, Channels, and Uses of Funds	9
	Budget Allocation, Execution, and Accountability	12
	Trends in Expenditures and Physical Inputs	16
	Summary of Findings	25
	Notes	26
Chapter 3	**School Performance and Output**	**27**
	Over-age Entry	27
	Promotion, Repetition, and Dropout	29
	Output Efficiency and Its Determinants	33
	Summary of Findings	35
	Notes	37
Chapter 4	**Service Quality and Outcomes**	**39**
	Teacher Knowledge	39
	Teacher Effort	40
	Teacher Practices and Behavior	42
	Teacher Incentives and Motivation	43
	Learning Outcomes	44
	Equity of Outcomes	45

	Summary of Conclusions	46
	Note	47
Chapter 5	**Reform Program and Financing Strategy**	**49**
	Government's Program and Financing Plan	49
	Critical Appraisal	52
	Conclusions	56
	Note	57
Appendix A	Tables	59
Appendix B	Quality of Service Delivery Survey	69
	QSD Survey 2014	60
Bibliography		71

Boxes

2.1	Problems in Executing the Budget for School Improvement Grants	14
3.1	Factors Responsible for High Student Repetition and Attrition	33

Figures

1.1	Focus Areas of the Report	6
2.1	Sources, Channels and Uses of Funds	11
2.2	Share of Education in Government Budget	12
2.3	Distribution of Schools by ORT Funds Received	16
2.4	Trends in Pupil Teacher Ratio (PTR) in Malawi	18
2.5	PTR by Standard (Grade) in Malawi, 2013	20
2.6	Distribution of Schools by PTR in 2014/15	20
2.7	Pupils Per Textbook	21
2.8	Distribution of Schools by Use of Math Textbook in Standard 5	22
2.9	Distribution of Schools by Use of English Textbooks in Standard 5	22
2.10	Proportion of Primary Schools with Classes Held in Open Air	24
2.11	Pupils-per-Classroom (Average in Standards 1 to 8)	24
3.1	Proportion of Over-Age Pupils	28
3.2	Rates of Progression (Without Repetition)	30
3.3	Promotion, Repetition and Dropout Rates in Std-1	31
3.4	Promotion, Repetition and Dropout Rates in Std-6	32
3.5	Repetition Rates by Standard	32
3.6	Distribution of Schools by Repetition Rate	34

| 4.1 | Time on Task in Classrooms | 42 |
| 4.2 | Proportion of Girls in Primary Enrollment | 46 |

Tables

2.1	Education Expenditure and Financing in Malawi, 2008–14	10
2.2	Sources, Channels, and Uses of Funds	11
2.3	Execution of Education Budget, 2011/12 to 2013/14	13
2.4	Execution of Budget for Priority Areas of Pooled Donor Support	15
2.5	Public Recurrent Expenditure on Primary Education (MK billion)	17
2.6	Sources of Growth in Primary Teachers' Salary Bill	19
2.7	Regional Primary Entry-Level Basic Monthly Salary Comparison, 2011	19
3.1	Mutual Inconsistency between Estimated Gross and Net Intake Rates	29
3.2	Comparison of "*Best Performing Schools*" with All Other Schools	35
3.3	Regression of P1 on Availability of Different Inputs	36
4.1	Basic Mathematical Skills of Primary Teachers	40
4.2	Teacher Absenteeism in Primary Schools	41
4.3	Negative Impact of Reported "Preparation Time"	41
4.4	Pass Rates in Learning Assessments, 2008 and 2012	44
4.5	Distribution of Pupils by Proficiency Level in Mathematics in 2012 (percentage)	45
4.6	Mean Scores in International Learning Assessments	45
5.1	Education Resource Envelope—Alternative Scenarios, 2013–18	50
5.2	Projected Composition of Education Expenditure, 2013–18	51
A2.1 (a)	Sources and Uses of Funds in Education, 2011/12	59
A2.1 (b)	Sources and Uses of Funds in Education, 2012/13	60
A2.1 (c)	Sources and Uses of Funds in Education, 2011/14	60
A3.1 (a)	Enrollment in Primary—Girls (Standard 1 to Standard 8), 2004/05 to 2013/1	61
A3.1 (b)	Enrollment in Primary—Boys (Standard 1 to Standard 8), 2004/05 to 2013/14	62
A3.1 (c)	Enrollment in Primary (Standard 1 to Standard 8), 2004/05 to 2013/14	62
A3.2 (a)	Repeaters in Primary—Girls (Standard 1 to Standard 8), 2004/05 to 2013/14	62
A3.2 (b)	Repeaters in Primary—Boys (Standard 1 to Standard 8), 2004/05 to 2013/14	63

A3.2 (c)	Repeaters in Primary (Standard 1 to Standard 8), 2004/05 to 2013/14	63
A3.3 (a)	Promotion Rates—Girls (Standard 1 to Standard 7), 2004/05 to 2012/13	63
A3.3 (b)	Promotion Rates—Boys (Standard 1 to Standard 7), 2004/05 to 2012/133	64
A3.3 (c)	Promotion Rates—Standard 1 to Standard 7, 2004/05 to 2012/133	64
A3.4 (a)	Repeater Rates—Girls (Standard 1 to Standard 8), 2004/05 to 2012/13	64
A3.4 (b)	Repeater Rates—Boys (Standard 1 to Standard 8), 2004/05 to 2012/13	65
A3.4 (c)	Repeater Rates, Standard 1 to Standard 8, 2004/05 to 2012/13	65
A3.5 (a)	Dropout Rates—Girls (Standard 1 to Standard 7), 2004/05 to 2012/13	65
A3.5 (b)	Dropout Rates—Boys (Standard 1 to Standard 7), 2004/05 to 2012/13	66
A3.5 (c)	Dropout Rates, Standard 1 to Standard 7, 2004/05 to 2012/13	66
A3.6	Coefficient of Efficiency in Primary, 2004/05 to 2012/13	66
A4.1	Results from SACMEQ II (2002) and III (2007) on Teacher Performance	67
A4.2	Average of Teaching Periods, 2011, 2012, and 2013	67
A4.3	Percent of Students with Textbooks (Classroom Observations), 2011 and 2012	67

Acknowledgments

The report was prepared by a team from the World Bank including: Vaikalathur Ravishankar (Consultant and lead author), Safaa El-Kogali (Lead Specialist), Deepa Sankar (Senior Education Economist and Task Team Leader), Nobuyuki Tanaka (Economist), and Nelly Rakoto-Tiana (Consultant). Special thanks to Safaa El-Kogali (Lead Specialist) and Sajitha Bashir (Practice Manager) for their guidance. The report benefited from comments forwarded by DFID in response to an earlier draft, and a process of internal review.

Malawi faces a significant challenge in attempting to improve the quality of primary education delivery in a context characterized by a significant contraction in domestically financed government expenditure. This challenge is compounded by uncertainty regarding future levels of external assistance. In light of these considerations, efforts to improve the quality of primary education in Malawi will require the identification of ways to more effectively utilize existing resources. This report is intended to make a contribution in this regard.

About the Authors

Vaikalathur Ravishankar is a consultant who retired from the World Bank in 2009 as a lead economist in the South Asia region. Based in New Delhi, he played a key role in developing policy-based lending to Indian state governments during 1998–2006. He has contributed to and led the production of numerous analytical reports, with a specialization in public expenditure analysis at the macro level and in specific sectors, fiscal federalism, and subnational economic growth diagnosis. He led several multidisciplinary teams and coordinated the Bank's lending program in the poor states, including in Uttar Pradesh and Orissa. He was the lead author of the Report titled "Orissa in Transition—Achievements & Challenges," November 2008 [Report No. 44612-IN]; and coauthor of *A Decade of World Bank Sub-national Policy-based Lending to India, in Indian Economy Sixty Years after Independence*, ed. R. Jha, Palgrave Macmillan, 2008. Since retirement, he has undertaken consulting assignments in Africa for DfID and the World Bank. He was the lead author of a DfID-sponsored Review of Public Education Expenditure in Ethiopia in 2010. He also co-authored "Subnational fiscal policy in large developing countries—Some lessons from the 2008–09 crisis for Brazil, China, and India," World Bank Policy Research Working Paper (2013).

Safaa El-Tayeb El-Kogali is the Education Practice Manager for the Middle East and North Africa region in the World Bank, based in Washington DC. She is a leading expert with 20 years of experience in international development. In her 13 years at the World Bank, Ms. El-Kogali has occupied a number of positions including Lead Specialist with the Education Global Practice, Sector Leader in Human Development for the Caribbean in the Latin America and Caribbean region, Senior Economist in the Human Development department and the Chief Economist's office in the Middle East and North Africa region, and Economist in the Education department of the Sub-Saharan Africa region. In addition to the World Bank, Ms. El-Kogali has also worked with the Population Council as Regional Director for West Asia and North Africa, based in Cairo, the Arab Republic of Egypt. She has also worked previously as a researcher with the Population Council and the Economic Research Forum (ERF) in Egypt. Her experience includes management, policy dialogue, research, and project design in over 15 countries. She authored a number of studies and recently published a book entitled: *Expanding Opportunities for the Next Generation: Early Childhood*

Development in the Middle East and North Africa. Ms. El-Kogali is a Sudanese national and has a Bachelor of Arts degree in Economics from the University of Pennsylvania, USA, and a Master of Philosophy degree with distinction in Development Studies from the Institute of Development Studies at the University of Sussex, UK.

Deepa Sankar is currently working as a Professor at the Center for Education Innovations and Action Research (CEI&AR) at the Tata Institute of Social Sciences, Mumbai, India. Deepa was a Senior Economist in the World Bank's education unit during February 2003–June 2015, working in South Asia region and Southern and Eastern Africa region. She was Task Team Leader for several education projects and Analytical and Advisory Activities in India, Sri Lanka, Malawi and Zimbabwe and had served as a regional coordinator for early childhood development-related work in South Asia. She has also worked in Afghanistan, Maldives, and Bangladesh, focusing on analytical activities. She has authored several papers on the economics and financing of education, education quality and school effectiveness and early childhood education. She has also carried out impact evaluation studies, learning assessment analysis and helped several countries in the regions she worked to set up Education Management Information Systems. She had also served as a member in several of the Expert Committees set up by the Ministry of Human Resources Development, Government of India to advice education policies and practices. Prior to joining the World Bank, Deepa worked as a faculty at the Health Policy Research Unit of Institute of Economic Growth, Delhi. Prof. Sankar holds an M.Phil. and Ph.D. in Economics received from Jawaharlal Nehru University, New Delhi, for her work carried out at the Centre for Development Studies, Thiruvananthapuram, Kerala, India.

Nobuyuki Tanaka works as an economist in the World Bank's Global Practice for Education. Based in Washington DC, he is currently leading Malawi Skills Development Project. He is also a task team leader for the Partnership for Skills in Applied Sciences, Engineering and Technology (PASET) initiative. Prior to the current assignment, based in Dar es Salaam, Tanzania, he provided technical and operational support to the government for their implementation of the Science and Technology, Higher Education Project (STHEP). He has been engaged in several analytical studies on education and skills. He holds a Ph.D. from Kobe University, Japan.

Nelly Rakoto-Tiana is a consultant with the World Bank's Global Practice for Education. She provides technical and analytical work for education projects in Africa. She has extensive experience working with complex data set, on designing and carrying out households surveys, and performing quantitative analysis. She holds a Ph.D. in Economics from Paris 13-University, France, coupled with certificate in quantitative and qualitative methods for advanced research in political economy and identification of the impact of public policies.

Executive Summary

Introduction and Objective

The objective of this report is to inform an improved understanding of expenditure allocations and processes, the quality of service delivery (QSD) in terms of inputs and outputs, and educational outcomes associated with primary education in Malawi. The report will also assess the government's own diagnosis of challenges in the primary education sub-sector, and the reform program intended to address them. The findings of this report are intended to inform discussions as to how to strengthen the government program and associated financing mechanisms, to enhance the likelihood of success. This report was initiated at the request of the United Kingdom (UK) Department for International Development (DFID).

The analysis contained in this report draws on primary data collected through a QSD Survey conducted in 2014/15, sponsored by DFID and managed by the World Bank. While the survey was intended to include a public expenditure tracking (PET) component, it failed to collect precise information on the flow of selected financial or physical inputs from the time of budget allocation through to the actual expenditure by the spending agency. This was partly due to time constraints created by weather-induced interruptions and partly due to the impact of the ongoing investigation into the *Cashgate* scandal on the willingness of officials to share precise financial information. On the other hand, the QSD survey gathered a wealth of data on input availability, teacher knowledge and effort, student absenteeism, etc. in a sample of 238 primary schools, based on classroom observations and interviews with both pupils and teachers.

An important feature of the analysis in this report is the use of the QSD survey data in conjunction with EMIS data for 170 schools that could be identified and matched between the two data sets. Multivariate regression analysis was applied to this combined data set to identify the determinants of output efficiency in primary schools. In addition, the report draws extensively on secondary data and existing studies on primary education in Malawi, including two sample surveys sponsored by the World Bank in 2011 and 2012; the Primary School Improvement Program (PSIP)—National Evaluation, 2011–13; a Public Expenditure Review carried out by the World Bank in 2013; and the United States Agency for International Development's (USAID) study on student repetition and attrition in primary education in Malawi published in September 2014.

Due to a lack of time series data with regard to the results of standardized tests administered to primary school pupils, this report does not attempt any statistical analysis of the determinants of learning outcomes. This analysis will be possible following the implementation of the Government of Malawi's (GoM) plan to institutionalize annual standardized testing of pupils' basic literacy and numerical skills in standards 4–8.

Context

Malawi has a population of approximately 16 million, of which 53 percent are below 18 years of age. As a landlocked nation with an economy characterized by a narrow export base and significant dependence on imports and foreign aid, its youthful population is one of Malawi's most precious assets. Delivering quality primary education to all 6–13-year-old girls and boys is of strategic importance for the country to take advantage of its demographic dividend and lift itself out of poverty. At the same time, it poses a big challenge precisely because the country is poor and resources are scarce while the numbers to be serviced are large. In 2013, per capita income in Malawi was US$270, and it ranked 174 of 186 countries surveyed by the United Nations Human Development Index. About 28 percent of the population was enrolled in primary education, higher than the 22 percent of 6–13-year-olds in the country, reflecting the persistence of significant over-age entry.

Malawi's economic performance has been volatile and vulnerable to external shocks. Steady economic growth of approximately 8 percent and a fairly stable fiscal environment between 2006 and 2010 were followed by a period of heightened fiscal imbalance, declining donor support, and a downturn in economic performance between 2011 and 2012. In 2012 the new government acted swiftly to arrest a growing economic crisis, enabling economic growth to recover to approximately 6 percent per annum. Allegations of financial impropriety, referred to as the "Cashgate" affair, arose in the last quarter of 2013, prompting some external donors to pull out of a pooled funding mechanism meant to support primary education and other social programs. This resulted in significant shortfalls in budget execution and increased recourse to costly domestic financing and public debt accumulation.

The Primary Education Sector

Education spending is relatively high in Malawi. Over the course of the past five years, public spending on education averaged 7 percent of gross domestic product (GDP), with private out-of-pocket expenditure estimated at 2–3 percent of GDP. Total education spending is higher than the regional average for sub-Saharan Africa. Primary education accounts for about half of education expenditure. Over 91 percent of primary schools are publicly financed. External resources contributed to 36 percent of all public education expenditure between 2008 and 2013.

The GoM has prepared an Education Sector Implementation Plan for 2013–18 (ESIP-II) in an effort to address widespread and persistent challenges with regard to high repetition rates, low completion rates (particularly for girls), poor rates of transition from primary to post-primary levels of education, and steadily worsening examination results. The plan integrates a significant emphasis on improving learning achievement in lower-primary education and on expanding access to secondary education. Given considerable uncertainty regarding future levels of external donor support for the education sector, ESIP-II presents three education financing scenarios for the 2013–18 period, corresponding with "low," "medium," and "high" levels of donor assistance, with expenditure for each education sub-sector and major components tailored in line with the three scenarios.

In the medium term, constrained fiscal space and continued uncertainty with regard to the level and composition of external assistance will limit the choices of government in pursuing universal access to primary education. The medium-term macro-economic framework developed by GoM for 2013–16 envisages a reduction in aggregate non-interest government expenditure by about 2 percentage points of GDP. In light of these contextual considerations, the GoM will need to focus more effort in extracting efficiency gains from the distribution and deployment of existing resources.

Key Findings

Expenditure

Government expenditure on primary education is progressive and pro-poor. The poorest quintile (20 percent) of the population accounts for 29 percent of the benefits of public spending on primary education while the highest income quintile accounts for 9 percent. In all other sub-sectors of the Malawian education system, the benefit incidence of government spending is regressive, and more than proportionately targeted at pupils from higher income families.

Despite the relatively large share of public expenditure allocated to primary education, outputs and outcomes remain poor. Challenges relating to high rates of absenteeism and repetition, and the high proportion of children who drop out of primary education are pervasive throughout the sub-sector. Just one in eight entrants to standard 1 will progress to standard 8 in the seven years envisaged for a full course of primary education. Student repetition rates of 20–25 percent for all pupils are particularly high in lower-primary grades, and 20 percent of girls currently repeat standards 5 through 8. Results of standardized international learning assessments by the Southern and Eastern African Consortium for Monitoring Education Quality demonstrate consistently poor performance on the part of Malawian primary school pupils for both reading and mathematics relative to the regional average.

The introduction of measures to devolve funding and decision-making to the school level has demonstrated a positive impact on the availability of non-personnel-related educational inputs. The PSIP, introduced in 2009, has been scaled up in a phased manner to cover all public primary schools. Subject to the approval of annual improvement plans submitted by each school, PSIP includes a School Improvement Grant (SIG), transferred directly to school bank accounts, for discretionary spending at the school level. A recent national evaluation of PSIP found that, despite significant systemic inefficiencies, PSIP has had a positive impact on the availability of non-personnel-related inputs in primary schools. However, the extent to which improved availability of inputs has contributed towards improved outputs and outcomes has not been assessed.

The vast majority of government expenditure on primary education is allocated to teacher salaries, limiting fiscal space for the procurement of critical non-recurrent educational inputs and capital expenditure. School teacher salaries have risen faster than per capita national income and are relatively high by African standards. The remuneration of teachers absorbs 84 percent of recurrent expenditure on primary education, with much of the remaining 16 percent absorbed through the payment of allowances to teachers. There is too little room for financing other inputs necessary for delivering quality education. The economic composition of expenditure will become more and more skewed if present practices and trends continue.

There are considerable delays in the process of approval and use of SIGs. Delays accrue as a consequence of the need for the District Education Manager to obtain approval from the District Councilor for the disbursement of funds. Poor communication with schools results in further delays in the withdrawal of funds from school accounts.

Pervasive weaknesses in accountability and the control of travel allowances lead to wastage and the abuse of funds. The cost of civil servants' travel in Malawi (equivalent to 4–5 percent of GDP) is much higher than in comparable countries. Teachers account for 40 percent of civil servants and an even higher share of travel allowances. High costs associated with travel are due, in part, to widespread abuse of the current system, including, *inter alia*, billing for unnecessary travel, inflated delegations, the collection of allowances without travel, the collection of multiple per diems for a single day, and the use of government fuel for private purposes. Rationalization and stricter monitoring of teachers' travel allowances could free up significant resources for non-salary recurring expenses, including school grants. Concerns relating to the abuse of, and poor standards of accountability with regard to, travel allowances were highlighted as an area of concern by the 2013 Public Expenditure Review.

Inputs and Utilization

Teachers are inefficiently allocated and are under-utilized, with significant variance across the sub-sector. The average pupil–teacher ratio (PTR) in Malawi is 69:1,[1] significantly higher than the national target of 60. High PTRs are repeatedly cited as justification for the hiring of additional primary teachers. However, analysis indicates that PTR varies greatly between grades and is most acute in the lowest grades of primary education where it averages over 100:1, as opposed to a PTR of 50:1 in standards 7 and 8. There is also considerable variation in PTR between schools, with the QSD survey demonstrating average PTR for standards

1–8 to be above 70 in one out of three schools; and less than 50 in two out of five schools. These findings buttress the view that significant space exists for more efficient use of the existing stock of primary teachers, without further adding to salary-related expenditure through additional recruitment.

Classroom shortages are acute and have a greater impact on educational outcomes than teacher shortages. While primary enrolment increased by 45 percent between 2004 and 2013, the number of primary classrooms rose by only 12 percent. Recent research sponsored by USAID identified classroom shortage as a primary factor contributing to student absenteeism, repetition, and dropouts. Lower-primary grades are taught in open air in one out of three schools, resulting in cancellation of classes due to rain and heat. Moreover, an analysis of schools with less than 5 percent repetition showed a statistically significant association with significantly better resource endowments, specifically in terms of classroom space.

Textbooks are poorly distributed and are not utilized effectively in class or by pupils at home. EMIS demonstrates that there are on average between 4 and 12 students per textbook, with the most acute textbook shortage experienced in grades 5 and 6. The results of the QSD survey, using a sample of 238 schools, indicated that in 40.3 percent of schools surveyed, no pupil enrolled in standard 5 was observed to be using a math textbook. Faced with uncertainty with regard to textbook supply, schools tend to stock up, using only a subset of available books on a daily basis. Moreover, students are not allowed to take textbooks home.

Output Efficiency

The enrolment of large numbers of over-age pupils in primary education undermines output efficiency of primary schools. The proportion of over-age pupils in standard 1 declined only slightly, from 56 percent to 49 percent, over the course of the past decade. Due to high rates of student repetition, over-age pupils are disproportionately concentrated in the higher grades of primary education. Over-age pupils are less likely to complete the cycle and more likely to drop out, due to shaming and harassment on the part of peers and teachers, and particular obstacles faced by pubescent female pupils due to poor water and sanitation facilities.

The primary education sub-sector in Malawi demonstrates persistently high rates of grade repetition, particularly in standards 1 and 2. According to official data, promotion rates in standard 1 increased from 43 percent to 55 percent over the course of the past decade. A rise in promotion rates is normally accompanied by a fall in both repetition and dropout rates. However, this is not the case in Malawi and repetition rates for standard 1 have remained stubbornly high at 25 percent, and around 20 percent, on average, across the first six grades of primary education.

Official data on enrolment, repeaters, and dropouts are mutually inconsistent, suggesting significant under-reporting by schools of the number of pupils who drop out of the system. By definition, rates of promotion, repetition and dropout must sum to 100 percent; however EMIS data do not fulfill this condition. It appears that dropouts are being under-reported; and those who are forever absent are kept on the rolls as repeaters the following year, most likely to inflate total enrolment.

The dropout rate from standard 1 in 2011/12, calculated residually from promotion and repetition rates, is 15.4 percent, which is much higher than the EMIS-based figure of 5.8 percent. Such a large discrepancy is cause for serious concern.

Approximately one quarter of schools demonstrate significantly lower rates of repetition. The most recent QSD survey found that 40 out of 238 schools have repetition rates of less than 10 percent at the lowest grades. Those schools are apparently making better use of school grants. Regression analysis across schools in the sample found that classroom space and non-salary funds received were statistically significant in explaining the variation in efficiency among schools, as measured by rates of promotion. Further research is required to identify all the schools that are performing much better than average, and to find out why, so that important lessons can be learnt for other schools to emulate.

Teacher Effort, Motivation, and Practice

The average teacher spends less than four hours per day in class. Classroom observations by the QSD survey team found teachers to be off-task for 20 percent in an average period, while 55 percent of observed periods was spent on passive learning or copying information from the blackboard. Only 25 percent of observed teaching periods were occupied with active teaching and learning activities, in the form of discussions, group work, activities, and answering questions.

Levels of teacher satisfaction and motivation are greatly influenced by school location and remoteness; and the most disadvantaged teachers in this regard are not being adequately compensated. The QSD survey found that 40 percent of interviewed teachers were happy with their work location. Of the 60 percent of teachers who were not happy with their place placement, the majority cited long distances between their homes and place of work as the primary reason. Monthly allowances intended to compensate teachers placed in remote locations are not being targeted to those most in need, with many teachers in the most remote locations not receiving the allowance, adding to poor levels of motivation. Remoteness also appears to reduce teachers' ability to redress their grievances.

Some types of teacher behavior contribute to poor educational outcomes. A recent USAID-sponsored study found that it was common for teachers to mock repeaters and over-age girls, who in some instances are encouraged to leave school and get married. The study also revealed that some teachers enter into sexual relationships with over-age girls, increasing the risk of early pregnancies and the spread of sexually transmitted diseases. Even in cases when improper teacher behavior is reported, this often only results in the offending teachers being transferred to another school, with little support given to victimized girls who are more likely to drop out of school as a consequence.

Financing Strategy

A highly concerning feature of GoM's current financial projections is that the share of expenditure in the education budget dedicated to servicing the salary bill is projected to rise even further. If the projected pace of additional teacher recruitment and consequent increase in the share of salaries in recurrent expenditure takes place, the scaling up of school grants under PSIP will not have adequate domestic financing. Such a crucial component will become highly dependent on the availability of external donor funding.

GoM's financing plan of the ESIP-II does not include off-budget donor funding of education projects. As a result of this omission, the plan frames the annual target of 1,500 additional classrooms for lower-primary grades as an 'aspiration' as opposed to a firm target with dedicated financing. Given that a shortage of classroom space is one of the most binding constraints affecting primary school performance, the omission of off-budget funding for basic education represents a serious weakness in the presented financial projections.

Conclusion and Recommendations

The ESIP-II is correctly orientated from a policy perspective, but envisaged interventions will not be sufficient to address deep-rooted and systemic problems such as low teacher morale and effort or lack of output orientation of schools. Moreover, the allocation of financial resources is not fully aligned with the needs of the system. The need for additional classrooms is receiving too little attention and finance in comparison with additional teacher recruitment, whereas the former is the more binding constraint to improving efficiency. Salaries and allowances are absorbing too large a share of available resources, squeezing the funds available for capital investments and for scaling up school grants as an effective instrument to improve service delivery.

In light of the constrained resource environment that is likely to frame efforts to improve the provision of primary education in Malawi in the medium term, recommendations focus on the leveraging of efficiency and productivity gains using available resources and inputs.

Measures to improve and enforce stricter monitoring of travel allowances could free up significant resources. The current system of extending allowances to teachers demonstrates features of widespread abuse. Accountability measures could potentially free up significant resources (probably as much as 0.5 percent GDP) for the funding of non-salary recurrent expenditure, including school grants.

Improving the distribution of the existing cadre of teachers across schools and grades will improve overall PTR and alleviate over-burdened teachers in lower grades without recourse to further teacher recruitment. A more nuanced and fiscally prudent approach is required to address teacher shortages. Reallocating teachers and their workload within and between schools is a cost-effective method of improving PTR that mitigates the need to hire additional teachers. Subject specialist teachers in standards 4–8, for example, could assist in teaching standards 1 and 2. The relative cost-effectiveness of improving the efficient use of existing teaching personnel, as opposed to recruiting additional teachers, is underscored by high personnel costs as a proportion of education expenditure, and the effect thereof in crowding out fiscal space for material inputs. In order to address acute PTRs in remote schools, MoEST may want to consider maintaining a pool of trained teachers for deployment to schools where needs are most acute.

The construction and creation of additional classroom space need to be targeted at the lower grades where classroom infrastructure is most inadequate. Schools should be encouraged to innovatively use SIGs to optimize available space, for example, through the erection of partitions to convert one large classroom into two smaller entities. Additional resources could be mobilized from external donors in support of classroom construction, targeted at schools that qualify on the basis of performance and need.

To improve the distribution and optimize the use of textbooks, the GoM could consider a public–private approach for promoting the development of local markets in which students can purchase textbooks so that they can take them home and use them in their spare time. This could be supplemented by a textbook grant, to be incorporated into the SIGs, to be used to ensure that poor students are able to afford textbooks. Over time, this system would allow for the development of a second-hand market for textbooks, reducing the net out-of-pocket expenditure borne by households.

There is a need to more effectively link school grant entitlements to school performance (for example, to promotion rates). The current practice of linking school grants to enrolment numbers generates perverse incentives for schools to maintain pupils who have virtually dropped out of the system on school rolls, and skews the attention of schools toward maximizing enrolment and away from improving the number of students who complete a full cycle of primary education with the desired levels of numeracy and literacy skills. The current proposal to link school grant entitlements to pupil–teacher ratios runs the risk of perpetuating, or worsening incentives for schools to inflate enrolment numbers. Moreover, measures must be taken to reduce delays in the disbursement of school grants and improve communication between districts and schools. The government's plan to release district grants conditional on the distribution of school grants to schools is a step in the right direction, as it will create incentives for district councils to reduce delays.

There is a need to undertake further research to feed into the process of policy making and mid-course corrections. Topics for further research include the following: (i) in-depth analysis of teacher allowances and how they may be restructured to improve teacher morale and motivation, and to incentivize more teachers to serve the lower grades where PTR is the highest; (ii) analysis of the performance of those schools exhibiting low repetition and high promotion rates, to find out why they perform better; (iii) a PET study focused specifically on SIGs, conducted in two phases, one immediately and the next after two years, to assess the impact of measures taken to cut delays and improve budget execution; and (iv) analysis of alternative options for designing the formula to determine the size of SIGs, so as to strengthen incentives for schools to maximize efficiency and effectiveness rather than maximize enrolment.

	Short Term (within 2 years)				Medium Term (3–5 years)			
Recommended Action	Time Horizon (years)	Expected Impact	GOM Current Plan	Recommended Action	Time Horizon (years)	Expected Impact	GOM Current Plan
Financial Management Measures								
Make disbursement of District Improvement Grants conditional on the prompt transfer of School Improvement Grants, by District Councils, to the school bank accounts	1	Improved execution of budget for school grants by reducing delays and avoiding misuse of funds meant for schools	Same action as recommended is being advocated by MoEST				
Limit further rise in the PE (regular salary) share of recurrent expenditure on primary education through better deployment of existing teachers and limiting numbers of new recruitment	Initiate immediately and sustain for 2 years	Protection of fiscal space for non-salary spending including school improvement grants	Recruitment of 19,000 additional teachers over next 2 years, implying significant further rise in PE share	Reduce salary share of primary recurrent expenditure to 80% by slowing down regular teacher recruitment and rise in pay scale	3–4	Increased fiscal space for material inputs and school grants; Reduced donor dependence for scaling up PSIP	ESIP-II scenarios project further rise in salary share till 2017–18, crowding out non-staff inputs
Rationalize and carefully monitor employees' travel, reduce unnecessary travel and frequency of meetings	Initiate in 1 year and sustain	Reduction in waste and misuse of public funds GDP	None				
Improve accounting of development spending and off-budget projects, classified by sub-sector and components	2	Improved alignment of resource allocation with policy goals	None				

table continues next page

	Short Term (within 2 years)			Medium Term (3–5 years)		
Recommended Action	Time Horizon (years)	Expected Impact	GOM Current Plan	Recommended Action	Time Horizon (years)	Expected Impact	GOM Current Plan

Education Sector Measures

1. Reform school grant formula

Recommended Action	Time Horizon (years)	Expected Impact	GOM Current Plan	Recommended Action	Time Horizon (years)	Expected Impact	GOM Current Plan
Replace enrolment in grant formula by "effective pupil years"	2	Remove adverse incentive to maximize enrolment. Reduce repetition not merely to 10% but even lower	ESIP-II advocates 10% cap on repetition and "need-based" entitlement of school grants, still linked to enrolment	Monitor and report on efficiency, and design "top up grant" targeted at resource-poor schools that improve their efficiency score	2–3	Strengthen output orientation Provide an ideal channel for additional donor support	

2. Rationalize teacher deployment and allowances

Incentivize standard 5–8 teachers to also teach standards 1–4 (non-monetary incentive)	1.5	Improved utilization of teachers within schools; reduction in excess burden in standards 1–4 and slack time in standards 5–8	ESIP-II proposes increasing school timing by one hour in standards 1–4	Rationalize teacher deployment across schools	2–3	Improved teacher availability in schools having most acute shortage (highest PTR)	ESIP-II proposes mandatory 2 years rural posting
Redesign rural posting allowances to ensure that teachers located in more remote locations receive larger amounts	1.5–2	Enhanced motivation and morale of teachers in the most remote locations		Rationalize entire package of pay and allowances to enable rewarding superior effort			Proposal to establish a transparent system of teacher promotions

table continues next page

	Short Term (within 2 years)			Medium Term (3–5 years)			
Recommended Action	Time Horizon (years)	Expected Impact	GOM Current Plan	Recommended Action	Time Horizon (years)	Expected Impact	GOM Current Plan
3. New textbook policy							
Pilot alternative public–private partnership approach to develop local markets for textbooks and limit public spending to subsidize only those who cannot afford to purchase books from the market	1–1.5	Improved utilization of textbooks in class and for home work	ESIP-II proposes piloting decentralized procurement by schools	Scale up new textbook policy	2–3	Development of second-hand market and reduction in net cost to households	Scaling up of decentralized textbook procurement by schools
4. Financing investment in classrooms							
Mobilize community contributions and external donor support for classroom construction	2	Increase number of primary classrooms, the input in most acute short supply	ESIP-II does not identify assured financing for classrooms				
5. Other measures							
Launch media campaign against over-age entry	1.5–2	Reduced over-age entry contributes to improved completion rates and internal efficiency	None				
Correct error in dropout numbers (estimate residually) and ensure school reporting is checked for consistency	2	Credible reporting of student flows and efficiency measurement	Not recognized by GoM				

Options for further strengthening the ESP-II program and improving the alignment of financial resources with policy priorities are summarized in the following Matrix of Recommended Actions.

Note

1. An average PTR of 69 is estimated based on current enrolment of 4.5 million. Current enrolment includes a large number of over-age pupils. This burden of over-age pupils on the education system is bound to decline over time. As teacher recruitment has long-term cost implications, the basis for hiring new teachers should be the population of 6–13-year-olds (3.5 million) instead of current enrolments.

Abbreviations

CBE	Complementary Basic Education
DEM	District Education Manager
DFID	U. K. Department for International Development
DSS	Direct Support to Schools Program
ECD	Early Childhood Development
EMIS	Education Management Information System
ESIP-II	Education Sector Implementation Plan for 2013–18
GDP	Gross domestic product
GDPmp	Gross domestic product at market price
GER	gross enrollment ratio
GIR	Gross intake rate
GoM	Government of Malawi
IHPS	Integrated Household Panel Survey
LDF	Local Development Fund
MANEB	Malawi National Examinations Board
MGWCD	Ministry of Gender, Women and Child Development
MLA	Monitoring Learning Achievement
MoEST	Ministry of Education, Science & Technology
NER	net enrollment ratio
NIR	Net intake rate
NLGFC	National Local Government Finance Committee
NSO	National Statistical Office
ODL	Open and Distance Learning
ORT	other recurrent transactions
PASS	Primary Achievement Sample Survey
PE	personnel emoluments
PET	public expenditure tracking
PSIP	Primary School Improvement Program
PSLCE	Primary School Leaving Certificate Examination

PTR	pupil-teacher ratio
QSD	Quality of Service Delivery Survey
SACMEQ	Southern and Eastern African Consortium Measuring Education Quality
SIG	School Improvement Grant
Std	standard (used interchangeably with grade)
SWAP	Sectorwide approach
TEVET	Technical Education, Vocational Education & Training
UK	United Kingdom
UNDP	United Nations Development Program
UNICEF	United Nations Children's Fund
USAID	United States Agency for International Development

CHAPTER 1

Introduction

Context

Malawi has a population of approximately 16 million inhabitants, with per capita income of approximately US$270 (2013). Malawi ranked 174 among 187 countries surveyed in the United Nations Development Program's (UNDP) 2013 Human Development Index. Approximately 85 percent of the population resides in rural areas, with livelihoods dependent on agricultural activities concentrated in the farming of tobacco and maize. As a landlocked nation with an economy characterized by a narrow export base and significant dependence on imports and foreign aid, Malawi is particularly exposed to external economic shocks. These economic considerations, in conjunction with policy uncertainty, have resulted in fluctuating economic growth, persistently high levels of poverty and periods of significant fiscal deficits.

Recent economic performance can be disaggregated into several distinct phases: Between 2006 and 2010, the country experienced steady economic growth of approximately 8 percent and a fairly stable fiscal environment. This was followed by a period of fiscal imbalance, declining donor support and a downturn in economic performance between 2011 and 2012. In May 2012 a new administration took office and acted swiftly to arrest a growing economic crisis. A number of successful economic policy interventions enabled economic growth to recover to approximately 6 percent per annum; however, the devaluation of the Kwacha, and the country's continued dependence on imports, have resulted in significant inflationary pressures. Inflation peaked at 38 percent in February 2013, but declined to below 20 percent in 2014.

During the years of relatively high economic growth (2006–10), there was a steady increase in aggregate government expenditure. High fiscal deficits, which had to be financed through borrowing from the domestic banking sector, arose during the period of economic contraction (2010–12) due to difficulties experienced in scaling back the magnitude of government spending. The macroeconomic framework of the Government of Malawi (GoM) for 2012–16 aims to advance fiscal sustainability through the strengthening of revenue mobilization, the restraining of growth in government expenditures, the clearing of payment arrears and the gradual repayment of loans to the domestic banking sector.

A scandal, popularly known as *Cashgate*, broke out in the last quarter of 2013, underpinning a fresh crisis in development financing.[1] Allegations of financial impropriety associated with the scandal resulted in several donors withdrawing their support for a pooled funding mechanism, which had been initiated as part of a Sector-Wide Approach (SWAp) for development financing. The withholding of external assistance, which the government had not expected, negatively impacted budget execution in 2013/14, including execution of the education budget.

In the aftermath of the scandal, the partnership between the GoM and external donors aimed at improving the performance of, and outcomes associated with, the education system is faced with a dilemma: International development partners want additional assurances from the GoM that aid will contribute to improved service delivery, and associated outcomes, before they restore previous levels of support. Concurrently, due to ongoing uncertainty regarding the level of short- to medium-term external assistance, as well as unresolved differences with regard to the mechanisms to be used to facilitate donor financing, the government is faced with significant challenges relating to the design and financing of development interventions. This report seeks to contribute to a diagnosis of the challenges facing the primary education sector and propose ways in which the government's reform program and sector financing strategy can be strengthened.

Demographic Dividend

In contrast to the developed countries of North America and Europe, and the emerging economies of Asia and Latin America, which face challenges associated with ageing populations and growing dependency ratios, Malawi stands to benefit from a growing labor force for most of the twenty-first century. Malawi's demographic transition began in the 1980s when the share of the population of working age as a proportion of the total population was approximately 49 percent. This ratio has risen gradually, reaching 52 percent in 2012, and is projected to peak at 64 percent toward the end of this century (Drummond, Thakur, and Yu 2014).

Universal access to basic education is widely acknowledged to be a key precondition for a country to take full advantage of the demographic dividend. An educated labor force enables countries to attract investment and transition to higher value-added production. From the standpoint of individual citizens, higher levels of education are associated with better pay and more stable employment. Moreover, improved educational outcomes enable more workers to find employment in the formal economy leading to improved productivity and rising incomes, with cumulative and positive implications for the expansion of a nation's tax base. The sustainable achievement of these outcomes requires the delivery of quality primary schooling to the population of children of school-going age. Recognizing the critical importance of expanding access to basic education, and the need to improve the quality of educational outcomes to meet the country's long-term development objectives, the GoM's national development strategy frames a context in which approximately 20 percent of the annual budget is dedicated to education.

Primary Education System

The population of children of primary school-going age (between the ages of 6 and 13 years) accounts for 22 percent of the total population of Malawi. Fewer than one in five of this age cohort were enrolled in primary school (standards 1 to 8 in Malawi) when the GoM abolished school fees for publicly financed primary schools in 1994. Primary enrolment has increased rapidly as a consequence of the abolishment of fees, rising from 1.8 million in 1993 to 4.5 million in 2014.[2] Due to the enrolment of high numbers of over-age, and some under-age, children in primary education, enrolment in 2014 was equivalent to 28 percent of Malawi's populace, higher than the share of 6–13 year olds in the total population.

The structure of the education system in Malawi is divided into the following sub-sectors: (i) basic education which, in turn, includes Early Childhood Development (ECD), primary education (standards 1 to 8) and Complementary Basic Education (CBE); (ii) secondary education (forms 1 to 4); (iii) Technical Education, Vocational Education and Training (TEVET); and (iv) higher education, which includes universities and professional training institutions. Public spending on basic education is predominantly concentrated in primary education, with ECD and CBE largely delivered by nongovernmental organizations with little or no public funding.

According to official data collected through the GoM's Education Management Information System (EMIS), in 2013 there were 5,405 registered primary schools in Malawi. The ratio of private schools has risen in recent years, from 3.6 percent in 2007 to 8.7 percent in 2013. Of the 91.3 percent of schools that are publicly financed, some are run by the government while others are managed by religious institutions using government grants. Following a decade of significant expansion, the number of public primary schools has grown on average at about 1 percent per year since 2009/10.

In order to improve the targeting of resources to those most in need, and to devolve decision-making closer to the schools, the GoM adopted a *National Decentralization Policy* in 1998. Enabling legislation, in the form of the *Local Government Act* of 1998, established 34 education districts (each district is divided into 10–20 zones) responsible for the delivery of primary education. The national Ministry of Education, Science & Technology (MoEST) retains overall responsibility for the education sector, with responsibility for supervision, quality assurance and the maintenance of primary schools devolved to District Councils. Primary Education Advisors were appointed and made responsible for supervision of and support to primary schools and the continuing professional development of teachers.

The GoM has initiated further devolution of educational responsibility, and funding mechanisms, through the adoption of policies to encourage community-led, school-based decision-making. The direct funding of primary schools was first initiated in 2006 under the Direct Support to Schools (DSS) program, which provided all schools, regardless of enrolment, with identical grants ($200) for the procurement of teaching and learning materials. The program was thereafter expanded to include support for costs associated with maintenance and rehabilitation, and the provision of funds was aligned with school enrolment. Despite its initial popularity, the DSS was considered to be too narrowly focused and insufficiently integrated within broader education and decentralization policy frameworks. As a consequence, DSS was progressively replaced by the Primary School Improvement Program (PSIP) between 2009 and 2013.

PSIP was initiated with support from the Education Decentralized Support Activity (a USAID funded agency), with the following objectives: (i) to ensure that all primary schools have management sub-committees; (ii) to improve community participation through parent–teacher associations and mother groups; (iii) to improve support to schools in the development of School Improvement Plans (SIPs) and to identify funding priorities; and (iv) to create bank accounts for all pilot schools to enable direct access to school grants. PSIP was initially piloted in six districts and was progressively rolled out to all of Malawi's education districts over the course of four years.

The expansion of the primary education sub-sector has absorbed a rising share of public resources, and has contributed to increasing allocations for the education sector as a whole. Public expenditure on education in Malawi has averaged just over 7 percent of gross domestic product (GDP) through the course of the past five years, significantly above the average for sub-Saharan Africa, with the primary education sub-sector accounting for 50 percent of recurrent expenditure on education in 2012/13. Despite more than 3 percent of GDP being spent on primary education, supply has been unable to keep pace with rising demand. The majority of primary schools are characterized by overcrowded classes, inadequate textbook provision, insufficient classroom infrastructure, and high pupil-teacher ratios, especially in the lower primary (1–4) grades. The condition of primary schools is generally worse in rural areas, and rural schools account for over 85 percent of enrolment.

Educational outcomes in Malawi are generally poor: Current statistics indicate that just one in three students who enter primary school will complete all eight years of primary education, and many students will take more than the scheduled eight years of instruction to complete a full cycle of primary education. Approximately 25 percent of grade 1 pupils, and 20 percent of students in grade 2, are required to repeat these grades, contributing to a situation in which only 19 percent of students progress to grade 8 without repeating a year.[3] A significant proportion of enrolled students demonstrate chronic absenteeism, and many drop out of the system altogether. These characteristics are informed by high levels of poverty, especially in rural areas, as well as inefficient service delivery, which cumulatively result in significant wastage of public resources.

Challenges associated with low levels of internal efficiency are compounded by the poor quality of education services delivered. The results of two recent national learning achievement studies demonstrate low levels of learning achievement with regard to language and numeracy, with almost 95 percent of pupils assessed in grade 7 demonstrating "no achievement" or "partial achievement" in mathematics in 2012. According to the Southern and Eastern African Consortium Measuring Education Quality (SACMEQ), Malawi ranks last in the region for grade 6 English reading, and second from last in mathematics.

Government's Response

In an effort to address widespread and persistent challenges with regard to high repetition rates, low completion rates (particularly for girls), poor rates of transition from primary to post-primary levels of education, and steadily worsening examination results, the GoM prepared an Education Sector Implementation Plan for 2013–18 (ESIP-II). The plan integrates a significant emphasis on improving learning achievement in lower primary education and on expanding access to secondary education.[4] The strategy for improving learning achievement in lower primary classes relies heavily on the strengthening of PSIP, including the provision of School Improvement Grants (SIG).

The medium-term macro-economic framework developed by the GoM is premised on a shrinking resource envelope, with an envisaged reduction in overall government expenditure of 3.5 percentage points of GDP between 2013 and 2016. In a context wherein the government has committed itself to reducing interest payments to 1.4 percent of GDP, noninterest-related expenditure in 2015/16 is expected to contract by just over 2 percentage points of GDP compared to 2012/13.

Malawi faces the challenge of improving the quality of primary education within the context of a significantly constrained domestically financed government expenditure. The magnitude of this challenge, from a policy, planning and budgeting perspective, is compounded by uncertainty with regard to levels of external assistance. Achieving and sustaining progress in expanding access to, and the quality of, primary education will require the identification of areas for improved efficiency and effectiveness in the utilization of available resources.

Objective and Scope

This report aims to inform and contribute to ongoing dialogue between the Government of Malawi and its development partners, through the diagnosis of the challenges confronting primary education in Malawi, and the generation of ideas for the further strengthening of the government's reform program and contingent financing strategies.

Figure 1.1 Focus Areas of the Report

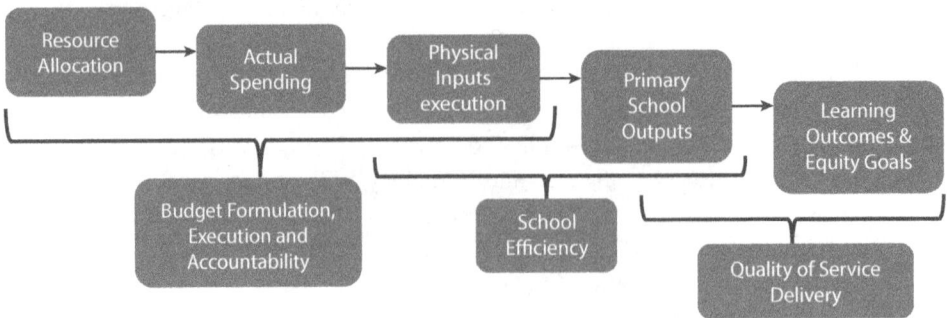

Source: World Bank.

The first focus area of the report will concentrate on the link between financial resources and physical inputs, taking into account budget formulation, budget execution and financial accountability (figure 1.1). Analysis will focus on how much money is spent on primary education, on what and by whom, and the identification of the most serious gaps between financial resourcing and the provision and utilization of educational inputs in primary schools.

Thereafter the report will move to an analysis of the link between physical inputs (teachers, textbooks, classrooms, etc.) and outputs (number of pupils completing each cycle), with a focus on the internal efficiency of the school system. In so doing, the analysis will attempt to answer the following questions: To what extent has Malawi progressed in enrolling all children of appropriate age in primary schools? What factors underlie high repetition rates and poor completion rates? Of the total number of schools that have received school grants, have some performed better than others, and if so why? Have some schools performed better despite resource constraints evident in other low performing schools? In answering the last questions, the analysis will attempt to identify examples of best practice that other schools can emulate.

A related, yet distinct, third area of analysis will focus on the link between teacher knowledge, effort, motivation and methods of teaching, on the one hand, and learning outcomes on the other. How, for example, are primary education services delivered with the available human and material resources, and what are the associated learning outcomes? Moreover, how equitable are current educational outcomes with respect to gender, regional and income dimensions?

Data Sources, Methodology, and Limitations

This report will draw on both primary and secondary data sources, including: (i) national accounts data, budget statements, quarterly and annual financial statements, time series data prepared by MoEST and the Public Expenditure Review study conducted by the World Bank in 2013; (ii) annual school level data covering 5,561 primary schools (2013) collected through EMIS; (iii) the Malawi

Integrated Household Survey (2011) and the Integrated Household Panel Survey (IHPS—2013), with a sample of 4,000 households; (iv) the Open and Distance Learning (ODL) Baseline survey of 2011, and a ODL follow-up survey conducted in 2012; (v) the Primary School Improvement Program Evaluation published in 2014, covering 715 schools; and (vi) the QSD survey of 2014.[5]

The report combines the standard method for conducting public expenditure reviews and analysis of trends relating to the internal efficiency of schools, using official national data, with statistical analysis of the determinants of school performance using the QSD survey data in combination with EMIS data. The attempt is to explain the variation among schools with respect to efficiency and other performance indicators by the variation in financial resources, physical inputs and teacher effort. Multivariate regression analysis has been used to analyze the determinants of output efficiency.

The QSD survey conducted in 2014/15 was intended to include a public expenditure tracking (PET) component. However, the study team failed to collect precise information on the flow of selected financial or physical inputs, from the time of budget allocation through to the actual expenditure by the spending agency. This was partly due to time constraints created by weather-induced interruptions and partly due to the impact of the ongoing investigation into the *Cashgate* scandal on the willingness of officials to share precise financial information. On the other hand, the QSD survey gathered a wealth of data on input availability, teacher knowledge and effort, student absenteeism, etc. in a sample of 238 primary schools, based on classroom observations and interviews with both pupils and teachers.

The QSD survey covered 238 schools selected through stratified random sampling from all the six divisions. A total of 16 schools were replaced on account of the following reasons, in order of importance: (i) they did not have all eight grades (the most common reason, accounting for 11 of the 16 cases); (ii) they were closed or nonexistent (four schools); and (iii) inaccessible (one school). The survey included interviews with officials at national and local (district) levels, with pupils and teachers in the selected schools as well as 40 minutes of observation of a standard 5 class in session.

Report Structure

Chapter 2 presents an analysis of budget allocations, actual expenditure and inputs at the school level. Gaps are identified and their significance discussed, with a focus on (i) budget execution, (ii) accounting and accountability, and (iii) efficiency with regard to the utilization of available resources.

Chapter 3 analyzes primary school performance and factors contributing to high levels of repetition and dropout, low rates of retention and waste in the utilization of public funds. In addition to describing trends in outcomes for primary education, this chapter examines variation in the performance of schools and attempts to isolate factors informing differential outcomes. EMIS data have been used in conjunction with QSD survey data for the purposes of a multivariate regression analysis of factors influencing school performance, as measured by rates of promotion from one standard to the next.

Chapter 4 examines factors that do not lend themselves easily to measurement, such as teaching quality, as well as factors that are measured less frequently and are not comparable over time, such as learning outcomes. Data collected through sample surveys are analyzed to examine the degree of teacher effort and issues affecting teacher morale and motivation. Equity in distribution of public spending is discussed, with respect to primary education and other sub-sectors of education.

Chapter 5 describes and critically assesses the government's reform program and financing strategy for education in general, and primary education in particular. This chapter synthesizes analysis from previous chapters to inform proposals to strengthen the reform program and its contingent financing strategy, to support the achievement of the government's objectives for primary education.

Notes

1. A scandal involving alleged misappropriation or theft of billions of Kwacha of public funds, allegedly through collusion between some private businessmen, ministers and senior bureaucrats.
2. Enrolment figures are from the Education Management Information System (EMIS), Government of Malawi.
3. All figures based on authors' calculations using EMIS data on grade-specific enrolment and repetition.
4. Education Sector Implementation Plan II: Towards Quality Education—Empowering the Schools.
5. Quality of Service Delivery Survey, 2014, sponsored by the UK Department for International Development (DFID) and managed by the World Bank; primary data were collected from a countrywide sample of 238 schools.

CHAPTER 2

Expenditures and Inputs

This chapter begins with a description of the sources and uses of funds in the Malawian education sector. This is followed by an analysis of budget allocations and actual expenditure, aimed at identifying challenges in budget execution affecting the delivery of primary education services. Moving from monies allocated and spent to actual goods purchased, the subsequent section of this chapter compares trends in different components of expenditure with physical inputs available in primary schools, including the number of teachers, textbooks and classrooms. Moreover, this chapter will also focus on weaknesses with regard to accountability and in the utilization of available resources, and concludes with a summary of the key findings.

Sources, Channels, and Uses of Funds

Public education expenditure is financed through a combination of domestic budgetary resources, grants from external donors, and concessional credits. The share of domestic and external resources for education averaged 63.5 and 36.5 percent respectively during the five-year period 2008/09–2012/13 (table 2.1). External donor support is channeled both through the national budget and through off-budget projects. On-budget external support can in turn be disaggregated into two categories: (i) support for priority areas of the national education budget through a Sector-Wide Approach (SWAp); and (ii) support to specific projects through the development budget.

Public resource allocation is channeled through four parliamentary votes: (i) the budget of the Ministry of Education, Science and Technology (MoEST), which supports the funding of personnel emoluments (PE), other centrally funded recurrent transactions (including centrally procured textbooks) and all on-budget development expenditure (Vote 250: 66.1 percent of Revised Budget in 2012/13); (ii) budgetary allocations to Local Assemblies/Councils covering a part of other recurrent transactions (ORT), including a portion of non-wage recurrent expenditure in primary education (Vote 701–754: 6.2 percent); (iii) "subventions" or government grants to public universities (Votes 275: 20.1 percent); and

Table 2.1 Education Expenditure and Financing in Malawi, 2008–14

MK billion	2008/09	2009/10	2010/11	2011/12	2012/13	2013/14
Public Education						
Expenditure	38.24	48.36	68.23	72.21	101.06	116.91
On-Budget	28.06	35.08	48.42	61.26	85.86	98.52
Domestic Financing	27.82	31.3	38.87	46.52	59.45	62.4
External Donor Financing[a]	0.24	3.79	9.55	14.74	26.41	36.12
Off-Budget Ext. Donor Support	10.18	13.27	19.81	10.95	15.2	18.39
Private out-of-pocket Exp[b]	n.a.	n.a.	15.57	n.a.	50.23	n.a.
Total Education Expenditure			83.8		151.28	
Memo items:						
GDPmp	553.82	761.94	881.40	1,056.85	1,415.18	1,809.22
Public Education Exp/GDP	6.9%	6.3%	7.7%	6.8%	7.1%	6.5%
Donor Share of Public Exp	27.3%	35.3%	43.0%	35.6%	41.2%	46.6%
Total Education Exp/GDP			9.5%		10.7%	
External On-Budget (US$mln)	1.71	25.98	54.60	65.50	89.53	98.22
External Off-Budget (US$mln)	71.81	91.02	113.21	48.65	51.51	50.00
MK per US$	141.78	145.82	175.00	225.00	295.00	367.80

Sources: (i) GoM, Financial Statements; (ii) Third Integrated Household Survey, 2011; and (iii) Malawi Integrated Household Panel Survey 2013.
Note: n.a. = not applicable.
a. Includes both budget support under SWAp and funding of discrete development projects.
b. Estimated from household surveys.

(iv) allocations to the Local Development Fund (LDF), to finance, *inter alia*, the construction of primary schools, classrooms and accommodation for teachers (Vote 272: 5.1 percent) (figure 2.1).

Public resources for education are also allocated through the budget of the Ministry of Gender, Women and Child Development (MGWCD) in support of ECD; however, this allocation is negligible in magnitude, and has been excluded from tables 2.1 and 2.2.

Local Councils are only responsible for the non-salary portion of recurrent expenditure with respect to primary schools. Salary payments are through direct transfers from the MoEST, which, moreover, procures key teaching and learning materials, such as textbooks, at the central level. District Education Manager (DEM) offices are responsible for school maintenance and the procurement of other goods and services, such as workbooks, chalk, and pencils. While the National Treasury communicates a ceiling for education sector resources to be transferred to the districts, the actual allocation is determined by the National Local Government Finance Committee (NLGFC).

Expenditures and Inputs

Figure 2.1 Sources, Channels, and Uses of Funds

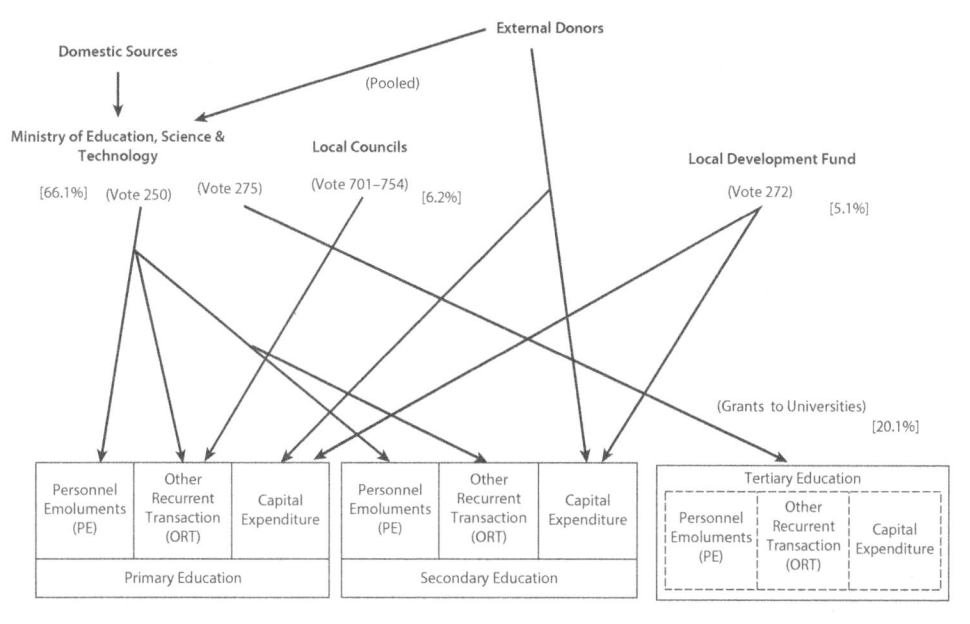

Source: World Bank.
Note: Percentage in parentheses refers to shares of revised budget in 2012/13.

Table 2.2 Sources, Channels and Uses of Funds

Sources	Uses / Channels	Primary Education	Secondary Education	Higher & Technical	Management
Domestic	Ministry of Education (MoEST)	PE & ORT	PE & ORT	PE	PE & ORT
External & Domestic	Local Councils	ORT			
Domestic	Subventions			ORT	
Domestic	Development Projects (Part 2)		Capital	Capital	
External	Development Projects (Part 1)	Capital	Capital	Capital	
External & Domestic	Local Development Fund (LDF)	Capital			

Source: World Bank.
Note: PE = personnel emoluments; ORT = other recurrent transactions.

At the local level, education infrastructure development (i.e., construction of classrooms, teachers' houses and associated infrastructure) is funded primarily through the LDF vote and implemented under auspices of the LDF's Community Window. Infrastructure development projects are supervised directly by local communities with guidance from DEMs and the local councils. Externally funded projects also contribute to capital investments in primary schools and teacher training centers.

Budget Allocation, Execution, and Accountability

The Government of Malawi (GoM) allocates close to 18 percent of its total budgetary resources to the education sector. In the 2014/15 national budget, education received the second largest sector allocation, surpassed only by agriculture. The share of resources allocated to education through the national budget has increased by 4 percent over the past 5 years from 13.4 percent in 2009/10 to 17.2 percent in 2013/14. (figure 2.2).

The national budget is approved at the beginning of the fiscal year (July to June in Malawi) and is revised mid-year following an assessment of revenue performance, inflation and other factors. Budget execution can be measured by comparing actual disbursements with the approved budget and/or revised budget allocations. The impact of double digit inflation in recent years has led to upward adjustments in the revised budget. In this context, it is more meaningful to use the ratio of actual disbursements to revised budget targets as the measure for budget execution.

The salary bill is the best executed component of the education budget, with shortfalls in budget execution consistently higher for development-related expenditure than recurrent expenditure (table 2.3). Within the allocation for recurrent expenditure, however, there is a consistent shortfall in the execution of budgets for Local Councils, which negatively affects the availability of material inputs in primary schools.

An analysis of budget execution in 2011/12, a year in which education-related budget execution achieved 96 percent of the revised target, demonstrates significant unevenness across supported components. The shortfall in budget execution

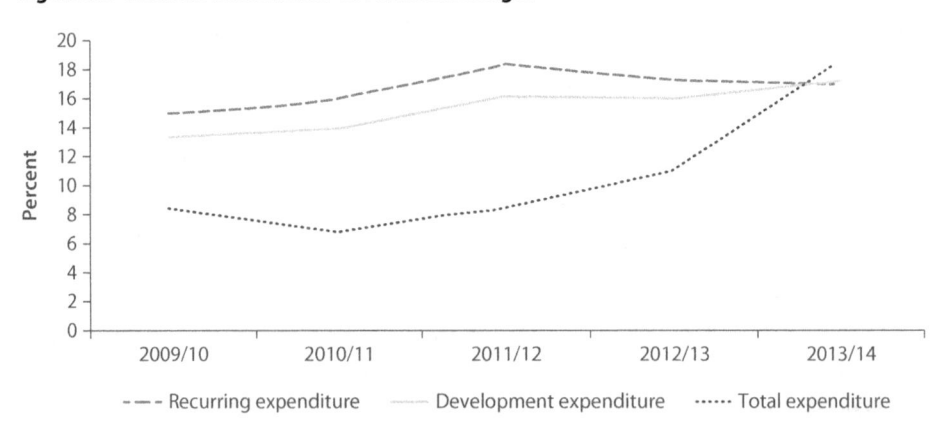

Figure 2.2 Share of Education in Government Budget

Source: World Bank.

Table 2.3 Execution of Education Budget, 2011/12 to 2013/14

MK Billion	2011/12		2012/13		2013/14	
	Rev Budget	% Spent	Rev Budget	% Spent	Rev Budget	% Spent
Sources/Chanells of Funds						
Recurrent Budget (Domestic & Pooled)	**53.46**	**99.9**	**76.68**	**100.4**	**101.76**	**85.0**
MoEST (Personnel Emoluments)	27.48	102.7	37.89	102.3	56.4	93.5
MoEST (Subventions to Higher Edn)	11.74	104.6	18.38	100.0	24.41	58.0
MoEST (ORT - Central)	10.08	94.0	14.64	102.3	12.82	95.8
MoEST (ORT - via Local Councils)	4.16	82.0	5.77	84.4	8.13	89.5
Resources for Development Budget	**10.1**	**77.9**	**11.5**	**77.2**	**20.12**	**29.8**
Dev Projects (Part II) - Pooled Funding	5.94	47.6	5.13	63.4	9.78	27.6
Local Development Fund (LDF)	3.51	100.0	2	226.0	5.88	29.2
Externally Funded Projects (Part I)	0.65	234.4	4.37	25.4	4.45	35.6
Total	**63.56**	**96.4**	**88.18**	**97.4**	**121.88**	**75.9**
Uses of Funds						
Primary Education (Recurring)	**27.24**	**89.6**	**38.07**	**101.1**	**45.2**	**93.1**
Regulary Salaries (PE)	19.95	99.9	29.04	101.4	35.4	99.4
Teaching & Learning Materials (Central)	3.13	50.2	3.26	116.9	1.67	92.7
Other Recurring Expenses (Districts)	4.16	69.7	5.77	90.3	8.13	65.7
All Other Sub-Sectors (Recurring)	26.22	110.6	38.61	99.7	56.57	78.5
Development Expenditure	10.1	77.9	11.5	77.2	20.12	29.8
Total	**63.56**	**96.4**	**88.18**	**97.4**	**121.88**	**75.9**

Source: Annual and Quarterly Financial Reports (from IFMIS), Finance Dept., MoEST.

was more severe in primary education than in other sub-sectors. Within primary education, salary payments were fully executed, while executed expenditure on textbooks (50 percent) and other recurrent costs (70 percent) fell significantly short of revised allocations. Improvements were demonstrated in 2012/13 when the revised allocation for primary education was fully distributed; however, of the non-salary-related resources channeled to the districts, which includes support for School Improvement Grants (SIGs), only 90 percent of funds were actually spent.

Budget execution deteriorated significantly in 2013/14, the year of the *Cashgate* scandal. Execution of devolved allocations for non-salary recurrent expenditure in primary education declined from 90 percent in 2012/13 to 66 percent in 2013/14 (table 2.3). Execution of the capital budget, including the execution of funds through the LDF which supports low-cost construction, fell to 30 percent.

While annual budget allocations for education under the Local Councils vote are meant to be equal to the allocation for non-salary recurrent expenditure in primary education (other than centrally procured materials), actual disbursement is unequal across the two line items. In 2013/14, for example, 89 percent of the education allocation to Local Councils was executed, compared to only 66 percent for non-salary recurrent expenditure in primary education. It is most likely that this disjuncture is a reflection of the gap between the amount transferred from central treasury to the districts, and the amounts approved by districts for primary education. This would corroborate the recent official finding that resources earmarked for education are spent on non-education-related items (see box 2.1). This practice, of which the MoEST is aware, is indicative of serious weaknesses in the current financial management system and must be addressed to mitigate the potential for delayed disbursement as well as the misallocation and abuse of education-related funds.

The annual education budget frames seven priority areas for support by a consortium of donors through a pooled fund aligned with a sector-wide approach (Education SWAp). MoEST reports demonstrate that budget execution in these priority focus areas deteriorated in 2013/14, although PSIP was a notable exception (table 2.4).[1] However, as explained above, the fact that

---

Box 2.1 Problems in Executing the Budget for School Improvement Grants

Following the approval of the national budget, Local (District) Councils receive monthly allocations from the Ministry of Finance. Monies are received in the form of a block grant for the aggregate funding of all supported activities in that month. Due to the fact that monies are collectively deposited into one bank account for each district, there is significant scope for the misallocation of funds earmarked for educational activities to support non-education-related spending. Moreover, while there are 34 education districts, there are only 28 district councils, resulting in instances whereby some education districts compete with one another for attention from the same district council (e.g., Mzimba North and South with the Mzimba District Council).

While the budget takes the form of a law passed by Malawi's Parliament, District Education Managers (DEMs) do not automatically access funds allocated in support of educational activities, such as PSIP. In practice DEMs must forward a formal request for payment to their district Director of Finance for approval. Thereafter, the district cash office will transfer funds to support School Improvement Grants from districts to school bank accounts dedicated specifically for PSIP.

According to the guidelines of the PSIP, all schools must draft a School Improvement Plan (SIP) articulating exactly how the school intends to spend the SIG. Following the formulation of the SIP at school level, they are then submitted to the DEM for consideration and (following recommended changes) approval in the form of a formal approval letter. Schools then take the approval letter to their bank and withdraw money from their PSIP bank account to fund the activities outlined in their SIP. In this way, the SIP can be considered the school's budget, with the SIG constituting the total amount of eligible funds that the primary school can spend.

Source: Primary School Improvement Program, National Evaluation Report 2010/11 to 2012/13.

Table 2.4 Execution of Budget for Priority Areas of Pooled Donor Support

Expenditure Components (MK billion)	2011/12		2012/13		2013/14	
	Revised Budget	% Spent	Revised Budget	% Spent	Revised Budget	% Spent
Construction and upgrading	7.81	72	7.51	92	1.37	57
Direct support to disadvantaged children	0.58	100	1.04	61	1.39	74
Textbooks & learning materials	3.57	70	5.10	88	3.47	39
Training of primary school teachers	2.56	80	3.56	94	2.97	69
Continued professional development	0.94	82	0.36	64	0.47	79
Primary School Improvement Program	1.38	23	2.29	82	4.34	95
Planning & financial management	0.42	47	0.31	82	0.05	52
Total	17.26	69	20.17	88	14.06	69

Source: MoEST Planning Department 2014.

MoEST succeeded in transferring 95 percent of the PSIP budget to the local level (table 2.4) disguises the fact that the districts failed to transfer the totality of these funds to school bank accounts within the fiscal year.

An official evaluation of PSIP reported that 80 percent of all primary schools received school grants in 2012/13. The more recent QSD survey found that 80 percent of schools surveyed had received some or all of the monies allocated to them in the form of SIGs in 2013/14 (Figure 2.3), with 57 percent of schools receiving between 600,000 and 700,000 Malawian Kwacha (US$1,600–1,900). The QSD survey moreover confirmed significant problems with regard to SIG budget execution. Specifically, the survey demonstrated that there are considerable delays on the part of the district Director of Finance in approving the disbursement of funds, as well as delays on the part of schools in accessing SIGs due to poor communication. Interviews conducted by the QSD survey team with DEMs revealed that it is not uncommon for transferred moneys to be left unspent for long periods of time because schools did not know that transfers had been made into their bank accounts.

Following the payment of salaries, the next best executed component of the education budget is the centrally managed ORT, or "other recurrent transactions" (table 2.3), the largest share of which is used to cover expenditure related to travel and other allowances received by teachers employed in government schools. The payment of allowances was highlighted by the recently published World Bank public expenditure review as being characterized by generally poor accountability mechanisms. At 4–5 percent of GDP, the annual cost of civil servants' travel is very high by global standards; and teachers constitute 40 percent of all civil servants. Allowances constitute a significant portion (23 percent) of

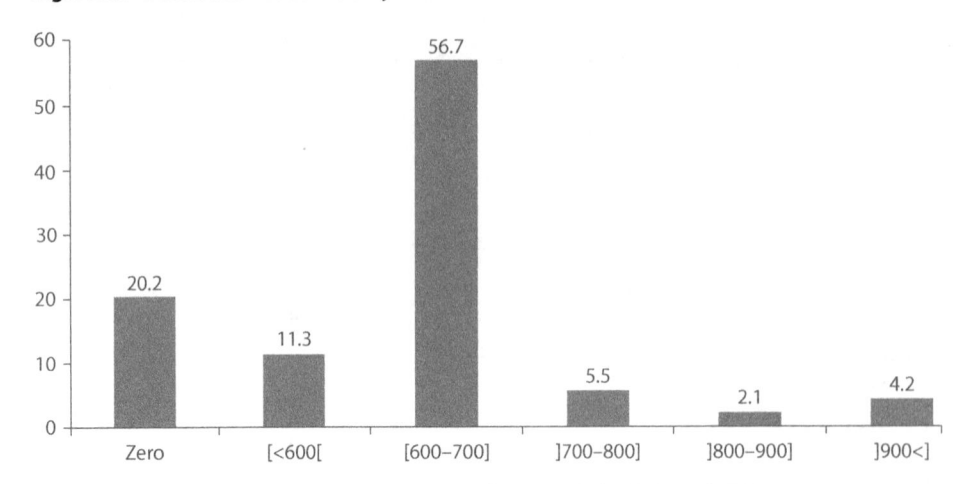

Figure 2.3 Distribution of Schools by ORT Funds Received

[Bar chart: Zero: 20.2; [<600[: 11.3; [600–700]: 56.7;]700–800]: 5.5;]800–900]: 2.1;]900<]: 4.2. X-axis: Funds other than salaries from MoEST (in thousand MK)]

Source: World Bank.

remuneration for civil servants in Malawi; and the payment of travel allowances is commonly perceived to constitute a supplement to salaries.[2] While available data do not enable estimating allowances specific to teachers, assuming it is at least 10 percent of salaries would imply that the share of teacher remuneration including allowances is more than 92 percent (rather than 84 percent as reported) of public recurrent expenditure on primary education.

High costs associated with travel are due, in part, to widespread abuse of the current system, including, *inter alia*, billing for unnecessary travel, inflated delegations, the collection of allowances without travel, the collection of multiple per diems for a single day, and the use of government fuel for private purposes.[3] Improved regulation and stricter monitoring of teachers' travel allowances could free up significant resources to fund non-salary recurrent expenditure, including school grants.

Trends in Expenditures and Physical Inputs

Public expenditure on education averaged 7 percent of GDP through the five-year period 2008/09 to 2012/13, of which 90 percent was allocated to recurrent expenditure and 10 percent to capital investment. Private out-of-pocket expenditure, incurred by households in support of education (including fees for secondary, technical and higher educational institutions), was estimated at 1.8 percent of GDP in 2010/11, and 3.5 percent in 2012/13. Total education spending, as a consequence, is estimated at approximately 9 percent of GDP, higher than many other African countries, including Kenya, Uganda, Mozambique and South Africa.[4]

Primary education in Malawi, consisting of eight grades (standards 1 to 8), accounted for 50 percent of recurrent government expenditure on education in

2012/13, and possibly a smaller share of development expenditure.[5] While primary education accounts for roughly half of off-budget donor-financed development projects, the majority of on-budget education development spending is allocated to the expansion of secondary education and teacher training colleges.

Table 2.5 demonstrates that public on-budget expenditure for primary education translated to approximately MK 9,350 per pupil (US$25) in 2013/14; representing, in real terms, a decline of 19 percent compared to the previous year. The share of expenditure incurred in the remuneration of staff, as a proportion of all expenditure in support of primary education, was 84 percent in 2013/14, up from 79 percent in 2006/07. The salary bill has grown faster than any other recurrent expenditure item, crowding out fiscal space for teaching and learning materials, maintenance and other recurring inputs. The non-salary component of recurrent spending, in real terms, exhibits a cyclical pattern: peaking in 2008/09

Table 2.5 Public Recurrent Expenditure on Primary Education (MK billion)

	2006/07	2007/08	2008/09	2009/10	2010/11	2011/12	2012/13	2013/14
Recurring Expenditure	11.15	12.55	15.74	14.34	21.32	24.41	38.47	42.08
Personnel Emoluments	8.81	9.65	11.78	12.72	18.16	19.94	29.45	35.19
o/w Teacher Salaries	8.12	8.89	10.85	11.72	16.73	18.37	27.14	32.42
Other Recurrent Transactions (ORT)	2.34	2.91	3.96	1.62	3.16	4.47	9.02	6.89
Memo Items:								
Enrolment in Std 1 to 8 (thousands)	3,281	3,307	3,601	3,670	3,869	4,034	4,189	4,498
Recur Exp per Pupil (MK at cur.pr)	3,400	3,796	4,372	3,907	5,512	6,051	9,184	9,356
Recur Exp per Pupil (MK at 10/11 pr)	4,646	4,806	5,091	4,196	5,512	5,622	7,037	5,694
Non-Salary per Pupil (MK at cur.pr)	714	879	1,100	440	818	1,107	2,153	1,532
Non-Salary per Pupil (MK at 10/11 pr)	975	1,113	1,281	473	818	1,028	1,650	932
Salary Share of Recurring Exp	79%	77%	75%	89%	85%	82%	77%	84%

Sources: (i) Financial Statements; (ii) EMIS; (iii) Bank staff estimates.

and 2012/13, and declining in 2013/14, to a level equivalent to MK 1,530 (US$4.20) per pupil per year.

Salary Expenditure and Teacher Numbers

The total salary bill for teachers in primary education grew, in nominal terms, at an average annual rate of 18.3 percent between 2004/05 and 2012/13. However, in spite of an increasing share of public resources being devoted to the salary bill, teacher recruitment lagged the growth in pupil enrolment until 2007/08 (figure 2.4). Over the course of the past five years, teacher recruitment has accelerated resulting in an improved pupil–teacher ratio (PTR).

At enormous fiscal cost, average PTR has been brought down to 69:1, a slight improvement on the PTR prevalent a decade ago. The gap between the rapid growth of the salary bill, and much slower growth in the number of teachers, is accounted for by high and rising unit costs associated with teachers. Disaggregation of growth in the salary bill demonstrates that (i) consumer price inflation accounted for 53 percent of growth in the salary bill over the past eight years; (ii) average real wage increases accounted for 28 percent; and (iii) growth in the number of teachers accounted for 18 percent (table 2.6). In other words, the growth of the salary bill, which has compromised the government's ability to allocate funds for other inputs critical for the delivery of quality primary education, has been driven predominantly by rising per-teacher salary, rather than by an increase in teacher numbers.

In terms of purchasing-power-parity, the basic salary for entry-level primary school teachers is relatively high compared to neighboring southern African countries (table 2.7). Malawi also ranks relatively high when taking into account the ratio of an entry level primary teacher's salary to average national income (GDP per capita), which is not unusual for countries with low levels of income.

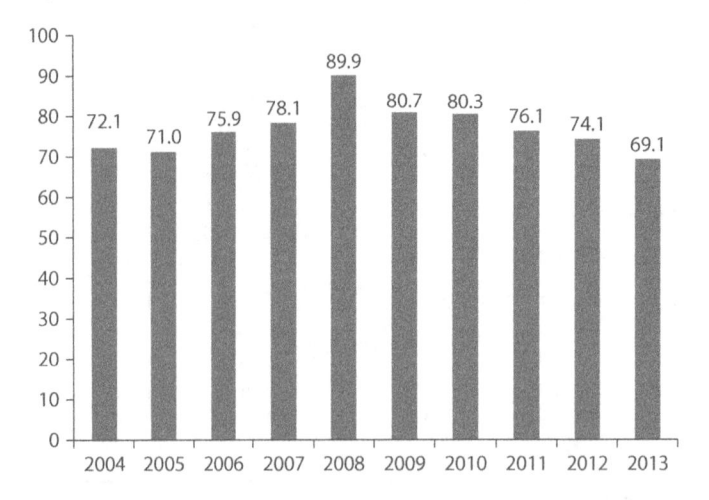

Figure 2.4 Trends in Pupil Teacher Ratio (PTR) in Malawi

Year	PTR
2004	72.1
2005	71.0
2006	75.9
2007	78.1
2008	89.9
2009	80.7
2010	80.3
2011	76.1
2012	74.1
2013	69.1

Source: EMIS 2013.

Expenditures and Inputs

Table 2.6 Sources of Growth in Primary Teachers' Salary Bill

	2004/05	2012/13	Average Annual Gth	Percent Contribution
Primary Teachers' Salary Bill (K Mln)	7,072	27,135	18.30%	
# Teachers (Standards 1 to 8)	43,952	56,534	3.20%	18%
Average wage per teacher	1,60,902	4,79,981	14.60%	
Average wage @ 2010 pr	2,50,638	3,67,757	4.90%	28%
Consumer Price Index	64.2	130.5	9.30%	53%

Sources: (i) Financial Statements; (ii) EMIS; (iii) Bank staff estimates.

Table 2.7 Regional Primary Entry-Level Basic Monthly Salary Comparison, 2011

Country	Local Currency	US Dollars	PPP US Dollars	Salary/GDP Per Capita
Kenya	KES 10,185	$115	$244	1.73
Malawi	MWK 24,813	$159	$393	5.61
Mozambique	MZM 6,579	$226	$416	6.62
Tanzania	TZS 196,500	$125	$360	2.86
Uganda	UGX 267,300	$106	$295	2.50
Zambia	ZMK 1,175,000	$242	$275	6.71

Source: World Bank.

Given these contextual considerations, and the fact that teachers employed in all sub-sectors of the education system constitute 40 percent of the civil service, it is not surprising that teachers are a well-organized interest group.

The shortage of teachers is acute in the lower grades of primary education (standards 1 and 2), with significantly better supply evident in the upper grades (figure 2.5). There are on average less than 40 students per teacher in standards 7 and 8, compared to a PTR of over 100:1 in standard 1 and 80:1 in standard 2. Significant variance in the distribution of teachers across grades implies that the current government policy aimed at achieving an average PTR of 60:1 across all eight grades of primary education misses the specificity of the challenge. In order to address the shortage of teachers in early grades of primary education, grade-specific recruitment of additional teachers and/or teaching assistants must target the recruitment for standards 1 and 2 where overcrowding is most prevalent.

Due to subject specialization in higher grades, it is expected that PTRs will be lower in upper primary grades (5–8) compared to lower levels of primary education. However, the differences in PTRs across primary school grades in Malawi are extraordinarily large, further buttressing the view that available resources are not being deployed effectively. The poor alignment of the distribution of teachers across grades also reflects the practice of promoting teachers to higher grades when the greatest teacher shortages are experienced in lower grades.

Variance in PTRs is evident not only between the lower and higher grades, but also between schools (figure 2.6). The QSD survey demonstrated that the average

Figure 2.5 PTR by Standard (Grade) in Malawi, 2013

- Std 1: 114.9
- Std 2: 85.9
- Std 3: 68.5
- Std 4: 61.1
- Std 5: 54.2
- Std 6: 45.4
- Std 7: 36.0
- Std 8: 25.7

Source: EMIS 2013.

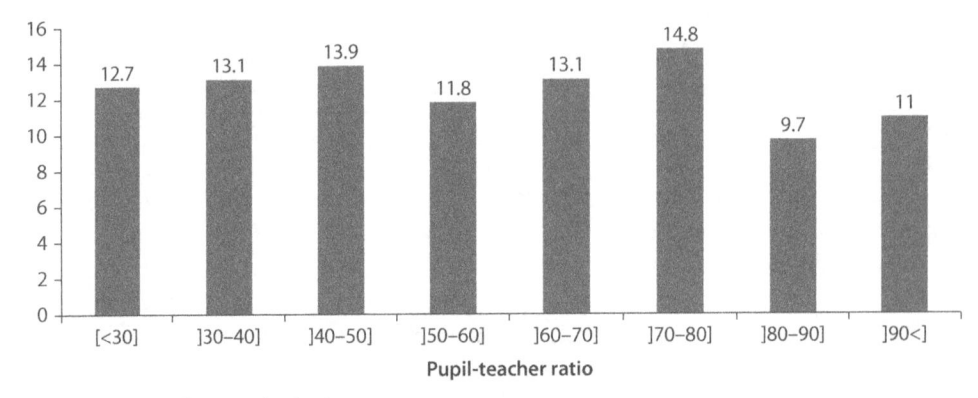

Figure 2.6 Distribution of Schools by PTR in 2014/15

- [<30]: 12.7
-]30–40]: 13.1
-]40–50]: 13.9
-]50–60]: 11.8
-]60–70]: 13.1
-]70–80]: 14.8
-]80–90]: 9.7
-]90<]: 11

Pupil-teacher ratio

Source: QSD survey of 237 sample schools.

PTR across all grades of primary education was lower than 40:1 in about 25 percent of the 238 schools surveyed.[6] Average PTRs ranged from between 40:1 and 70:1 in about 40 percent of schools, and above 70:1 in the remaining 35 percent of schools surveyed.[7] These findings suggest that (i) current teacher deployment is driven by various factors, including teacher preference, that distort efforts to address the most acute shortages; and (ii) there is considerable scope for easing PTRs through the redeployment of teachers between schools.

In the short to medium term, a context in which it is likely that resources for education will be constrained, significant gains can be achieved through improving the alignment of teacher supply with school needs. Reallocating teachers and their workload within and between schools is a cost-effective method of improving PTR that mitigates the need to hire additional teachers. Subject specialist teachers in standards 4 to 8, for example, could assist in teaching standards 1 and 2. The relative cost effectiveness of improving the efficient use of existing teaching personnel, as opposed to recruiting additional teachers, is underscored by high personnel costs as a proportion of education expenditure, and the effect thereof in crowding out fiscal space for material inputs.

For the past 20 years, growth in primary enrolment and high PTRs have been used to justify the continued recruitment of teachers. When, in times of heightened fiscal stress, the government has proposed temporarily freezing teacher recruitment, external donors have cited high primary school PTRs to motivate for the further recruitment. Evidence of significant inefficiencies in the use of the current stock of schools teachers underscores the need to re-examine this challenge. The evidence presented here suggests that efforts to improve total teaching time, and the reduction of PTRs, can be achieved through the improved use of available teaching resources, without increasing the number of teachers.

Non-Salary Expenditure and Material Supplies

As noted earlier, the expenditure item labeled "Other Recurrent Transactions" (ORT) contains a variety of items, only some of which can legitimately be classified as the purchase of goods and services. ORT includes, *inter alia*, allowances for personnel, many of which move in alignment with the salary bill. This trend indicates that the crowding out of fiscal space for material supplies is more pronounced than ORT expenditure implies.

Challenges with regard to the supply and distribution of textbooks are acute: EMIS data demonstrate that the average textbook is shared by between 4 and 12 students with the most acute shortages experienced in standards 5 and 6 (figure 2.7). Moreover, the results of the recent QSD survey demonstrate that the actual utilization of textbooks by students in classrooms lags the EMIS

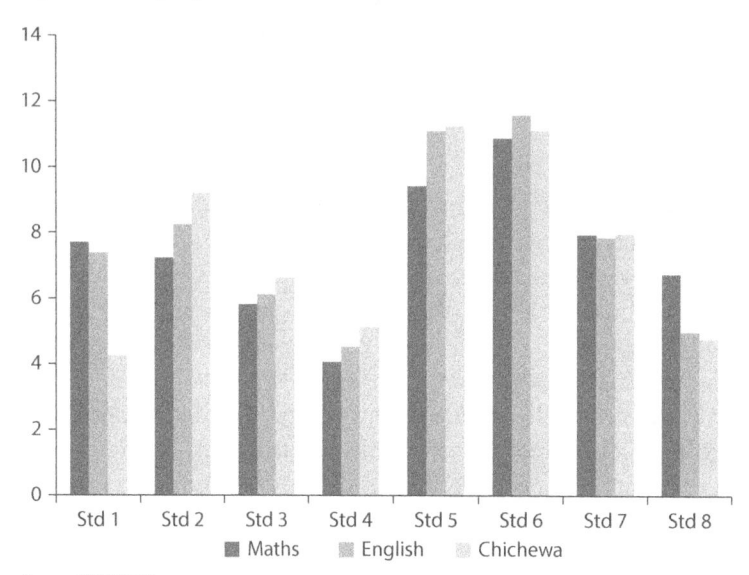

Figure 2.7 Pupils per Textbook

Source: EMIS 2013.

Figure 2.8 Distribution of Schools by Use of Math Textbooks in Standard 5

Percentage of pupils having math textbooks in class	Percent
0	40.3
]0–5]	15.5
]5–10]	6.6
]10–15]	5.0
]15–20]	6.6
]20–25]	2.8
]25–30]	4.4
]30–40]	3.9
]40–50]	6.1
]50–60]	2.2
]60<]	6.6

Source: QSD survey 2014.

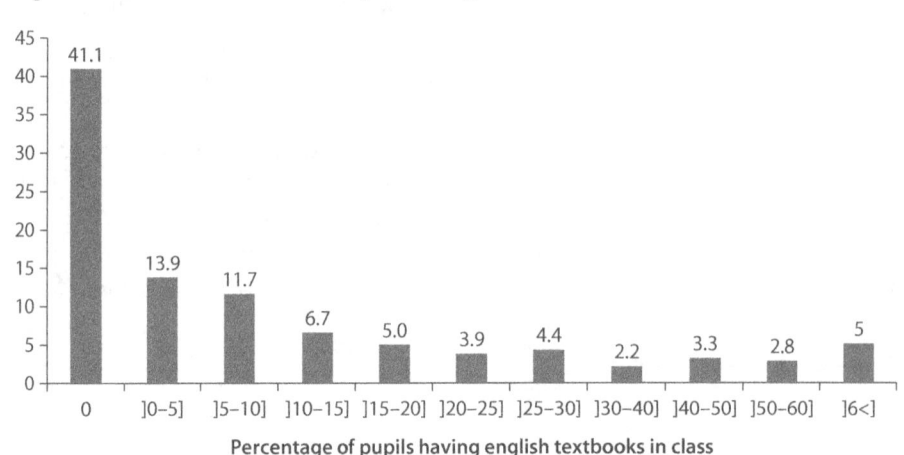

Figure 2.9 Distribution of Schools by Use of English Textbooks in Standard 5

Percentage of pupils having english textbooks in class	Percent
0	41.1
]0–5]	13.9
]5–10]	11.7
]10–15]	6.7
]15–20]	5.0
]20–25]	3.9
]25–30]	4.4
]30–40]	2.2
]40–50]	3.3
]50–60]	2.8
]6<]	5

Source: QSD survey 2014.

pupil-per-textbook ratio (figures 2.8 and 2.9). While EMIS data reflect the number of enrolled pupils divided by the number of textbooks available within a school, the QSD survey collected data on the actual number of books observed in the students' possession in the classroom. The results of the QSD survey indicate that in 40.3 percent of schools surveyed, no pupil enrolled in standard 5 was observed to be using a math textbook (figure 2.8).

The disjuncture between EMIS and QSD data suggests that only a portion of the supply of textbooks distributed to schools are actually used during lessons, with the remainder being kept in cupboards, presumably for future use. The data demonstrate another case of sub-optimal utilization of available resources, with significant scope for improvement.

The poor utilization of available textbooks is a phenomenon observed not only in Malawi but in many countries dependent on externally funded international procurement for school textbooks due to a poorly developed domestic publishing and printing industry. It is commonly observed that when schools are not assured of a regular and timely supply of textbooks, a portion of available materials are kept in store for future use. Moreover, when official policies determine that textbooks are provided free of charge, and that schools are required to ensure that each textbook is used for a minimum of three years by successive cohorts, pupils are often prevented from taking textbooks home, limiting the utility of textbooks for student learning.

In an effort to address issues relating to textbook supply and distribution, the MoEST is considering interventions to devolve the procurement of textbooks to the school level. Critical outstanding questions relate to how a devolved system of textbook procurement will assure the local availability of textbooks, and how schools will finance the annual purchase of textbooks on a recurrent basis. An additional option, with potentially more positive implications for sustainability, would be for MoEST to pursue a public-private model in which textbooks are distributed to licensed private bookstores for onward sale to students. A portion each school's SIG could be used to subsidize pupils who are too poor to afford the cost of textbooks. A distinct advantage of selling textbooks to students is that it enables pupils to take textbooks home for study outside of the classroom. Over time, this system would allow for the development of a second-hand market for textbooks, reducing the net out-of-pocket expenditure borne by households. An additional advantage associated with this model of textbook distribution is that when students/households pay for textbooks, they are likely to value them more highly and maintain them in better condition. Textbooks maintained in good condition are more likely to be sold at a good price on the second hand market, and less likely to be spoilt or lost compared to freely distributed materials.

Capital Expenditure and Classroom Availability

A weakness associated with the current system of financial accounting in the Malawian education system is that there is no disaggregation of the development budget and actual capital expenditure by sub-sector (basic, secondary, TEVET, and higher education), and expenditure related to teacher training and administrative support. Challenges in this regard are magnified by the absence of similarly disaggregated data with respect to off-budget donor-assisted projects. However, reliable data demonstrate a serious shortage of primary school classrooms: While the stock of primary school classrooms increased from 37,000 to 41,500 between 2004 and 2013, representing a real increase of 12 percent, primary enrolment rose by 45 percent over the same period.

EMIS data suggest that in approximately 33 percent of primary schools, all standard 3 pupils are taught in open air, with a marginal improvement to 30 percent for pupils in standard 4 (Figure 2.10). A major disadvantage associated with outdoor teaching is that classes are cancelled in the event of rain and when it is deemed to be too hot. Pupils in standards 7 and 8, in which cohorts are generally smaller, and PTRs are of a lower magnitude, are generally taught in classrooms, many of which were built to accommodate 100 pupils or more. These practices reflect poor optimization of the use of existing classroom space, due to the fact that in higher grades, in many instances, fewer than 50 pupils occupy a room large enough to accommodate twice that number.

The poor supply of classroom infrastructure was identified by a 2014 study by USAID as one of the primary factors contributing to high rates of student absenteeism, repetition and attrition.[8] While the government has repeatedly set ambitious targets for classroom construction, financing has been inadequate to address the backlog in school infrastructure, and the average ratio of pupils to classrooms has deteriorated through the course of the past decade (figure 2.11). Similar to

Figure 2.10 Proportion of Primary Schools with Classes Held in Open Air

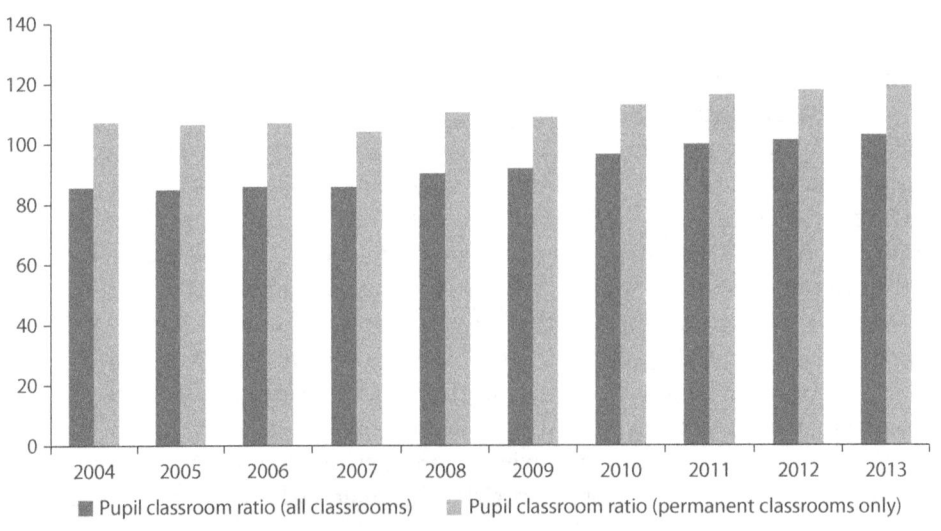

Standard	Percent
Std 1	21.80
Std 2	23.70
Std 3	34.20
Std 4	31.70
Std 5	22.30
Std 6	14.20
Std 7	6.80
Std 8	3.40

Source: EMIS 2013.

Figure 2.11 Pupils-per-Classroom (Average in Standards 1 to 8)

■ Pupil classroom ratio (all classrooms)   ■ Pupil classroom ratio (permanent classrooms only)

Source: EMIS 2013.

the case of teacher supply, the challenge is greatest in the lower grades and government efforts need to be concentrated in this area. Schools should be encouraged to innovatively use SIGs to optimize available space, for example through the erection of partitions to convert one large classroom into two smaller entities.

Summary of Findings

The composition of public spending in support of primary education in Malawi significantly undermines the effectiveness of interventions to improve the system. Too large a share of financial resources is consumed by teacher salaries and allowances, leaving little fiscal space for the procurement of other inputs necessary for the delivery of quality education. Salaries constituted 84 percent of recurrent public expenditure on primary education in 2013/14, and the wage bill will rise in the forecast period in the absence of measures to reform current practices of teacher recruitment in support of averaged PTR across all eight primary grades. In order to address mushrooming costs associated with recurrent expenditure in support of salaries, and to more effectively address acute teacher shortages in a minority of schools and in the lowest grades, a more effectively targeted and fiscally prudent approach must be formulated and implemented.

The multiplicity of factors contributing to the disjuncture between the allocation of funds and their actual use in delivering primary education services, include: (i) relatively high, and increasing, unit costs of teachers, inclusive of regular salaries and allowances that in many instances are perceived to be salary supplements; (ii) the inefficient allocation and utilization of teachers employed within the primary education sub-sector that results in an excessive teaching burden for some teachers (particularly in the lower grades) and light workloads for others; (iii) weaknesses with regard to accountability and control of travel costs; (iv) weaknesses and delays in the execution of budgets to support non-salary recurrent expenditure devolved to local authorities; and (v) inadequate investment in additional classroom infrastructure.

The complexity and interaction of these problems will necessitate action on the part of multiple authorities and stakeholders. There is need for the Ministry of Finance to prioritize interventions to strengthen financial management and accountability through, *inter alia*, the implementation of more effective controls with regard to travel allowances, fiscally prudent management of wage adjustments, and the implementation of measures to improve the execution of locally devolved budget allocations. The MoEST must take the lead in setting realistic and focused targets with regard to PTR and pupils-per-section ratios, implementing policy changes to improve the efficiency of teacher distribution across schools, to improve textbook distribution and to optimize the use of textbooks by students. School management committees and head teachers need to be empowered to improve, and must take steps towards improving, the allocation and enhanced utilization of available resources within schools, including teachers, material aids and classroom space.

Notes

1. Budget execution declined in 2013/14. Three development partners of the original five in the pooled fund (DfID, Germany and UNICEF) pulled out of it in September 2013 because of *Cashgate*.
2. Malawi Public Expenditure Review, The World Bank, 2013.
3. Ibid.
4. UNESCO Education Statistics 2011.
5. Development expenditure on education is not classified into primary, secondary and other sub-sectors in Malawi's financial accounts.
6. QSD survey 2014.
7. Even when the average PTR is less than 40:1, the ratio may be as high as 60:1 in standard 1.
8. Report of study on student repetition and attrition in primary education in Malawi, USAID, September 2014.

CHAPTER 3

School Performance and Output

The performance of the primary school system can be assessed through a consideration of (i) the extent to which appropriately aged children enter the system; (ii) the proportion of entrants who complete the eight-year cycle of primary education in line with the intended schedule; (iii) the proportion of children who complete a full cycle of primary school education who demonstrate the acquisition of skills associated with this cycle; and (iv) equity in the distribution of benefits across gender and income groups. The first three of these considerations must be optimized for the achievement of the goal of universal primary education. This chapter will focus on universal entry and output efficiency. The quality of service delivery learning and equity outcomes are evaluated in the next chapter.

Over-age Entry

The official recommended age for entry into standard 1, the first year of primary school in Malawi, is six years of age. However, the total number of children who enter standard 1 each year is far higher than official estimates of the number of six-year-olds in the country, reflecting the large number of over-age entrants to the system. However, the proportion of over-age pupils in standard 1 has declined slightly over the course of the past decade, from 55.8 to 49.4 percent (figure 3.1), and over-age students constitute a larger share of enrolment in higher grades, due to enforced repetition as a consequence of students not passing tests administered at the end of each grade.

Research suggests that over-age pupils are more likely to drop out of school before completing a full cycle of primary education. A report on student repetition and attrition in primary education in Malawi noted that over-age students are often laughed at by their younger counterparts, causing them to withdraw from school-related activities. This contributes to higher levels of absenteeism and poor concentration in class, and, in turn, comparatively high levels of truancy, and children dropping out of the schooling system altogether.[1]

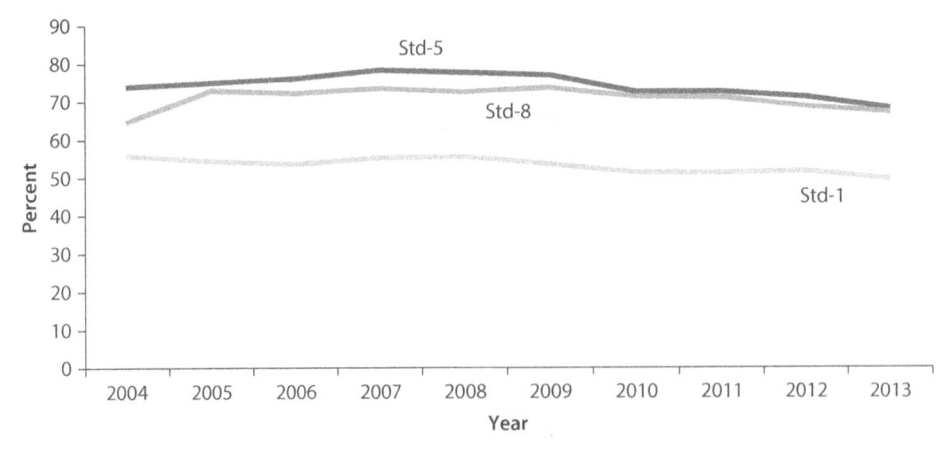

Figure 3.1 Proportion of Over-Age Pupils

[Line chart showing percent of over-age pupils from 2004 to 2013 for Std-1, Std-5, and Std-8. Std-5 remains around 75-78%, Std-8 around 68-73%, and Std-1 declining from about 65% to around 50%.]

Source: World Bank.

A factor contributing to the persistence of over-age entry in Malawi is the relative remoteness of rural schools and reluctance on the part of parents to allow six-year-olds (especially girls) to walk long distances to and from schools, especially if they are not accompanied by an older sibling. In 15 of 34 educational districts, the average distance between households and the nearest school is more than 4 kilometers. Moreover, in approximately half of Malawian school districts, up to 30 percent of schools are inaccessible during the rainy season, a factor that is more pronounced in rural areas.

Based on official age-specific population statistics, the MoEST estimated a net intake rate (NIR) for standard 1 of 96 percent of six-year-olds in 2013/14; implying that only 4 percent of children at the official age for entry to school did not commence primary school that year. However, the credibility of the NIR is undermined by an officially estimated gross intake rate (GIR) of 171 percent.[2]

Trends in officially estimated NIR and GIR are mutually inconsistent: By comparing the first and third rows of table 3.1, estimates of NIR indicate that through the course of the past seven years, over 90 percent of six-year-olds enrolled in standard 1 each year. The number of six-year-olds who did not enroll at the official age for primary school enrolment is illustrated in the fifth row. Summing the population of potential late entrants since 2007/08 yields a figure of 161,415 children, which is less than half of the reported 349,410 over-aged entrants reported in standard 1 in 2013/14.

The most plausible explanation for the discrepancy demonstrated in table 3.1 is that age-specific population figures are significantly under-estimated. If we assume that the actual population of six-year-olds is 10 percent higher than official estimates, NIR and GIR would be 87 and 156 percent respectively. These are not mutually inconsistent, and probably closer to the truth. If it is true that the population of six-year-olds has been under-estimated, this implies that Malawi has further to go before declaring success in achieving the first step towards universal

Table 3.1 Mutual Inconsistency between Estimated Gross and Net Intake Rates

	2007/08	2008/09	2009/10	2010/11	2011/12	2012/13	2013/14
Memo: Pop(6) - NSO	4,00,398	4,12,934	4,25,861	4,37,868	4,48,787	4,58,050	4,63,332
Gross Intake in Std 1	6,39,149	6,65,590	6,73,506	6,90,578	7,05,553	7,45,149	7,94,209
o/w those aged 6	3,64,362	3,79,899	3,91,792	4,20,353	4,26,348	4,39,728	4,44,799
o/w wrong age	2,74,787	2,85,691	2,81,714	2,70,225	2,79,205	3,05,421	**3,49,410**
Those aged 6 out of school	36,036	33,035	34,069	17,515	22,439	18,322	
Cumulative 6+ out of school							**1,61,415**

Sources: Education Management Information System (EMIS); National Statistical Office (NSO).

primary education – namely, the enrolment of all six-year-olds in standard 1. The Net Enrolment Rate (NER) and Gross Enrolment Rate (GER) for primary education—estimated at 87 and 135 percent in 2013/14 respectively—are likely to be lower, perhaps by as much as 10 percent. Moreover, there are more 6–13 year olds who are out of school than the official estimates suggest.

Challenges associated with over-age entry to primary school require serious attention. Long-term solutions will require improvement with regard to transporting children to school and/or the building of more schools of smaller size to make educational services more accessible for rural and remote communities. Interventions for implementation in the short-term could include effective communication campaigns on the advantages of early entry in school. Another option could be to divert significantly over-age students (more than two years above the recommended age for each grade) into a separate stream for "*adult children*," who could be taught at a different time of day. The streaming of significantly over-aged pupils into a dedicated track would help to mitigate the peer-related challenges outlined earlier that undermine the retention of over-aged pupils in Malawi. However, this option is probably too expensive and beyond the financial capacity of the government at this time.

Promotion, Repetition, and Dropout

Students entering standard 1 in any particular year can be disaggregated into three categories in the subsequent year: (i) those who are promoted to standard 2; (ii) those who repeat standard 1; and (iii) those who drop out of school altogether and are no longer considered to be enrolled. Rates of promotion, repetition and dropout in standard 1 are defined as follows:

$P1_{12/13}$ = Rate of Promotion from 1 to 2 (2012/13) = Those promoted to Std-2 in 2013/Enrolment in Std-1 in 2012, where

Those promoted to Std-2 in 2013 = Enrolment in Std-2 in 2013 − Repeaters in Std-2 in 2013;

$R1_{12/13}$ = Rate of Repetition in Std-1 (2012/13) = Repeaters in Std-1 in 2013/Enrolment in Std-1 in 2012; and

$D1_{12/13}$ = Rate of Dropout from Std-1 (2012/13) = [Enrolment in Std-1 in 2012 − Those promoted to Std-2 in 2013 − Repeaters in Std-1 in 2013]/ Enrolment in Std-1 in 2012.

For the purposes of analysis, in each year the following should hold true: P1 + R1 + D1 = 1 (or 100 percent). However, the EMIS data on grade-specific enrolment, repeaters and dropouts do not fulfill this condition. For example the 2013 EMIS reports 53,659 dropouts in standard 1 and 925,452 as the total number of students enrolled in standard 1 in the previous year (2012), implying that D1(2011/12) = 5.8 percent. However, EMIS figures for enrolment and repetition in standard 1 yield a P1 (2011/12) of 61.4 percent and an R1 (2011/12) of 23.2 percent. The sum of P1, R1 and D1, based on this EMIS data, equals 90.4 percent when it ought to be 100 percent.

Inconsistencies evident in the EMIS data relating to student flow imply suboptimal checking and quality assurance with regard to data reported by schools. For the purpose of the analysis in this chapter, it is assumed that the number of students that drop out of the system is underreported. Underreporting of dropouts is the most likely explanation for the evident discrepancies in the data, as it is less likely that schools underreport enrolment or repeater numbers, due to the presence of these students in schools. Based on this assumption, dropout rates have been calculated residually (D = 1 − P − R). As a consequence, D1 (2011/12) has been recalculated as 15.4 percent, against the EMIS based figure of 5.8 percent.

Rates of progression have improved over time but remain extremely low (figure 3.2). As recent as in 2012/13, uninterrupted progression rates to standard 5

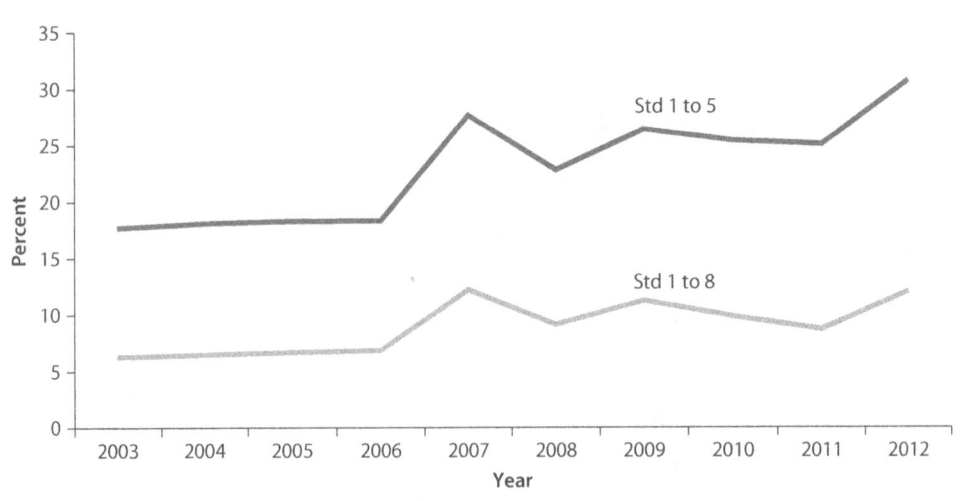

Figure 3.2 Rates of Progression (Without Repetition)

Source: EMIS data on enrolment and repeaters by grade.

and 8 were as low as 31 and 12 percent respectively. This means that less than one in three pupils enrolled in standard 1 in 2012 will reach standard 5 in 2016; and less than one in eight students enrolled in standard 1 in 2012 will reach standard 8 in 2019. The balance of students will either complete the sub-cycle following more than eight years in primary school, or they will drop out prior to completion of a full course of primary education.

Promotion rates for standard 1 increased from 55 percent in 2003/04 to 65 percent in 2012/13 (figure 3.3). While this is certainly good news, a rise in promotion rates is normally accompanied by a fall in both repetition and dropout rates. This trend is not evidenced at the lowest primary grade in Malawi with repetition rates for standard 1 remaining stubbornly high at 25 percent. This phenomenon is more pronounced in standard 6 where the promotion rate rose from 72 to 75 percent between 2003 and 2013, but the repetition rate similarly increased from 12.4 to 15.4 percent across the same period (figure 3.4]).

In Malawi, on average 25 percent of new entrants to primary education repeat their first grade. The average rate of repetition in the first six grades is above 20 percent, significantly higher than the African average of 15 percent. Grade repetition has remained persistently high, and has demonstrated a slight increase over the past decade (figure 3.5), in spite of government efforts to mandate automatic promotions for selected classes. Persistently high rates of repetition are associated with several factors operational at the household, community and school levels (box 3.1).

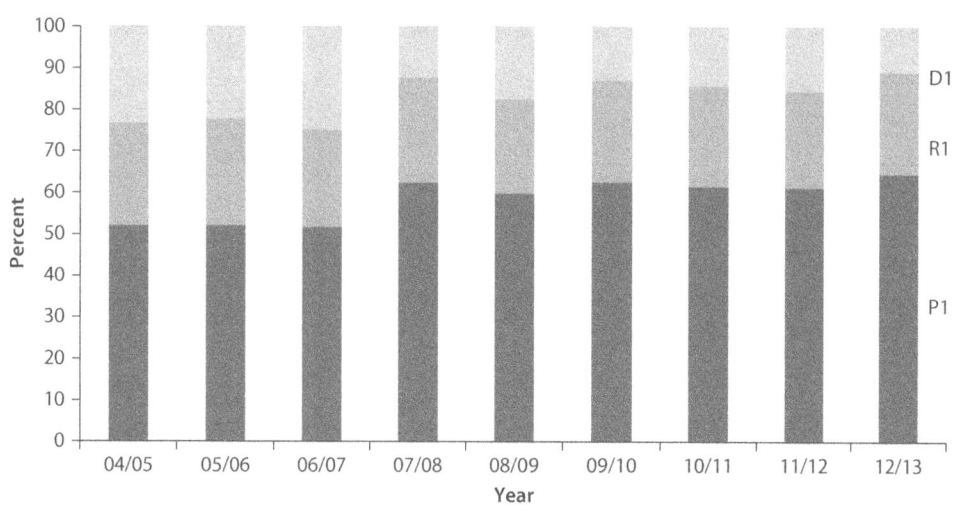

Figure 3.3 Promotion, Repetition and Dropout Rates in Std-1

Source: Calculated from EMIS data on grade-specific enrolment and repeaters.

Figure 3.4 Promotion, Repetition and Dropout Rates in Std-6

Source: Calculated from EMIS data on grade-specific enrolment and repeaters.

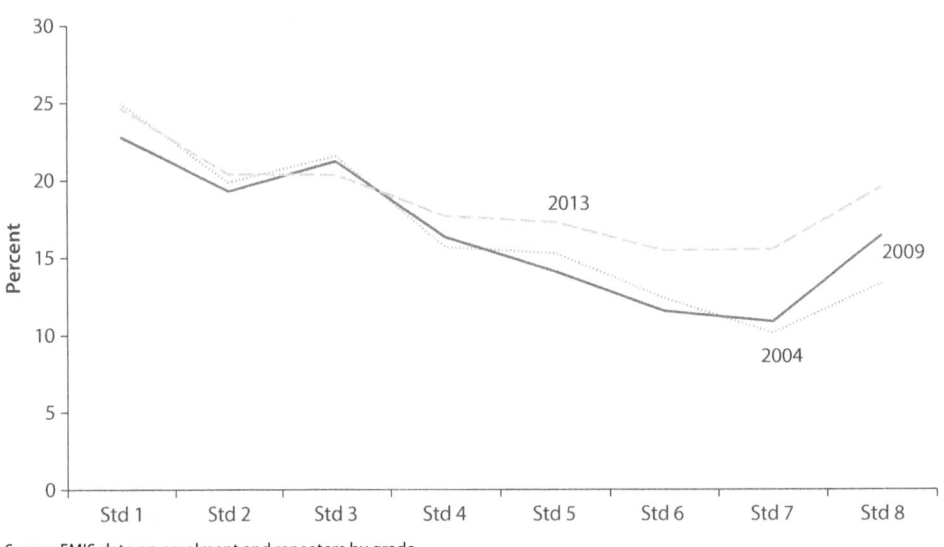

Figure 3.5 Repetition Rates by Standard

Source: EMIS data on enrolment and repeaters by grade.

A school-level factor that could affect the accuracy of data collected is that schools may be exaggerating the numbers of students repeating lower grades in order to maximize entitlements to school grants. Rather than recording a pupil who enrolled, but was rarely present in class, as a dropout, the current system may incentivize schools to record these students as repeaters.

Box 3.1 Factors Responsible for High Student Repetition and Attrition

Household Level
- Subsistence livelihoods in which children are expected to contribute to household chores and wage earning work.
- Children miss classes on market days.
- Low levels of educational attainment on the part of parents.

Community Level
- Cultural practices—Initiation ceremonies that can disrupt two to three weeks of a school term.
- Community Video Centers, which contribute to truancy as children leave school to watch films.
- Concerns relating to the safety of children, specifically girls, during their commute to school, linked to distance from the school.

School Level
- Lack of learning in school—75 percent of student repeaters felt they did not learn much in class.
- Teacher absenteeism—students enrolled in early grades receive only 2–3 hours of teaching per day.
- High student-teacher ratio—combined with absenteeism and low teaching time by those present.
- Ineffective teaching—37 percent of teachers admitted that poor teaching was responsible for repetition; and 43 percent of repeater students said they did not understand lessons in class.
- Poor school access—Long distance prevents attendance during rainy and cold seasons.

Source: USAID Study 2014.

The GoM recognizes that the *"high current repetition rate in primary education is not effective at improving students' learning achievement, is wasteful and ultimately financially unsustainable."*[3] A 2011 government circular stated that repetition rates should be reduced through the capping of repetition at 10 percent of pupils per class. Data suggest that this circular had little practical impact on the ground, and the objective of the circular has been restated as a priority in the ESIP-II.

This chapter buttresses the view that the determination of funds distributed through school grants needs to be reformulated to more effectively align the funding of SIGs with school performance, and to mitigate distortions introduced through the current practice of linking grants to enrolment numbers. The ideal measure of school performance is learning achievement, as measured by standardized tests of literacy and numeric competency levels. While this practice may be implemented in the medium-term, as the GoM institutionalizes standardized testing on an annual basis, in the interim, the formula for determining school grant amounts could be improved through the use of "effective pupil-years" (explained below) instead of total enrolment.

Output Efficiency and Its Determinants

Internal efficiency, or "output efficiency," in primary schools is measured by distinguishing between pupil-years that result in promotion and those that result in repetition or dropout. From a public policy perspective, pupil-years that do not result in promotion constitute a waste of resources, due to the inputs consumed not achieving the desired output.

The coefficient of efficiency for each primary school, and the system as a whole, may be defined as:

C (Primary) = Effective pupil-years/Total pupil-years in standards 1–8, where
Total pupil-years = Enrolment in Std-1 + Enrolment in Std-2 +… + Enrolment in Std-8; and
Effective pupil-years = [Enrolment in Std-1 × P1] + [Enrolment in Std-2 × P2] + … + [Enrolment in Std-7 × P7] + [Enrolment in Std-8 × P8], where P8 = Proportion of students enrolled in std-8 who pass the national examination.

Using the formula defined above, the coefficient of output efficiency for all primary schools in Malawi has improved from 65 to 73 percent over the course of the past decade. While this represents a notable improvement, the most current coefficient of output efficiency implies that 27 percent of current public resources deployed in primary education are spent on pupils who do not attain the expected level of learning.

Moreover, the positive trend in the average level of output efficiency disguises considerable variation across all schools. The fact that some schools are doing much better than others is encouraging with important implications for policy formulation. Observations in 203 schools, as part of the QSD survey, demonstrated that taking all primary grades together, 11.8 percent (24 of 203) of schools demonstrated repetition rates of less than 5 percent, while 7.9 percent (16) schools had repetition rates of between 5 and 10 percent (figure 3.6).

A comparison of the 24 schools with less than 5 percent repetition with all other schools in the sample, demonstrates that schools with low rates of repetition are associated with significantly better resource endowments, specifically in terms of classroom space (table 3.2). Differences between the two sub-sets of

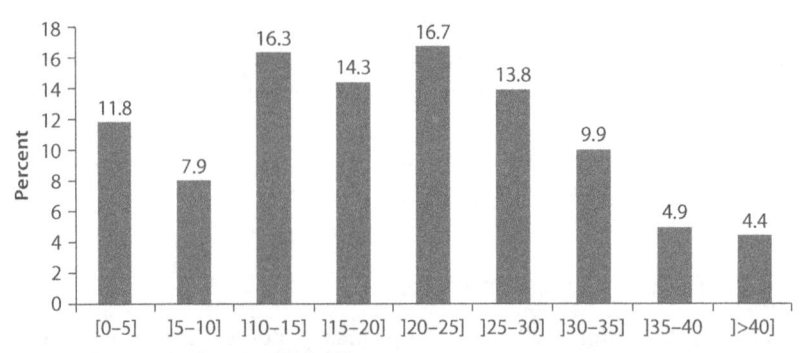

Figure 3.6 Distribution of Schools by Repetition Rate

Range	Percent
[0–5]	11.8
]5–10]	7.9
]10–15]	16.3
]15–20]	14.3
]20–25]	16.7
]25–30]	13.8
]30–35]	9.9
]35–40]	4.9
]>40]	4.4

Source: QSD survey 2014 (among 203 schools).

School Performance and Output

Table 3.2 Comparison of *"Best Performing Schools"*[a] with All Other Schools

Characteristics of primary schools	Repetition rate	
	<5%	>5%
Variables from PET- QSD survey (2014/15)		
Average pupil-teacher ratio	64	69
Average pupil-classroom (rooms built to be a classroom)	100	123
Average pupil-room (total rooms, built, provisional or make-shift)	73	92
MoEST non-salary funding (in thousands, 2013/14)	513	488
Other funding (in thousands, 2013/14)	108	137
Number of schools	**24**	**179**
Variables from EMIS (2013/14)		
Average pupil-English textbook ratio, Grade 1 to 7	3	4
Average pupil-Chichewa textbook ratio, Grade 1 to 7	3	3
Average pupil-Math textbook ratio, Grade 1 to 7	4	4
Number of schools matched with EMIS database	**22**	**174**

Sources: (i) QSD survey; (ii) EMIS.
a. "Best performing" in this table refers to schools with average primary repetition rate of less than 5 percent.

schools with regard to PTRs and pupil-textbook ratios were not statistically significant in explaining the variation in repetition rates across schools.

Regression analysis using the QSD survey data and EMIS data for 170 schools in the sample demonstrates that at the lowest grade, i.e., standard 1, the availability of classrooms and the amount of funds available for non-salary recurrent expenditure both have a statistically significant impact on the promotion rate (table 3.3). While the availability of classrooms had a significant impact, neither the availability of teachers (PTR) nor the availability of subject textbooks was demonstrated to be a significant explanatory factor for variations in school performance. The absence of an association with textbook availability may be due to the lack of variation in textbook usage in the sample. In the vast majority of schools surveyed, very few textbooks were observed as being used in classrooms (table 3.3), as discussed in chapter 2.

The coefficient of pupils-per-classroom is –0.039 in the regression displayed in table 3.3, which means that unit reduction in this ratio improves the promotion rate in standard 1 by 0.039 percentage points. Suppose an additional classroom improves pupils-per-section in standard 1 from 120 to 60. Other things remaining unchanged, this would improve the promotion rate by (60 times 0.039 =) 2.34 percentage points, which is quite insignificant compared to the rate of progress in average promotion rates observed in recent years.

Summary of Findings

The primary education system in Malawi suffers from persistent over-age entry with negative implications for the probability of pupil survival and completion,

Table 3.3 Regression of P1 on Availability of Different Inputs

	Promotion rate Grade 1
Primary pupil–teacher ratio 2013/14	0.037
	(0.05)
Pupil-English textbook Grade 1, 2013/14	0.155
	(0.18)
Pupil-Chichewa textbook Grade 1, 2013/14	−0.095
	(0.25)
Pupil-math textbook Grade 1, 2013/14	−0.066
	(0.13)
Pupil-classroom Grade 1, 2013/14	−0.039***
	(0.01)
Funds other than salaries from MoEST (in thousands), 2013/14	0.012***
	(0.00)
Constant	58.750***
	(4.35)
Observations	170
R^2	0.144

Source: QSD survey 2014.
Notes: (i) Standard errors are in parentheses; (ii) *$p<0.1$, **$p<0.05$, ***$p<0.01$.

and concurrent negative implications for output efficiency. The negative effects of variable age underscore the need for the GoM to take steps to reduce the wide variation in age at entry in standard 1. Potential interventions in this regard could include: (i) the immediate implementation of communication campaigns advocating the entry of children into primary school at appropriate age; and (ii) over the medium term, provision of additional smaller schools closer to remote and underserved communities.

Promotion rates between standards 1 and 2 have increased from 43 percent to 55 percent over the course of the past decade. While this is good news, this trend should have been accompanied by a reduction in both repetition and dropout rates, which has not been the case. Repetition rates for standard 1 have remained stubbornly high at 25 percent.

Dropout numbers aggregated by EMIS are of an order of magnitude significantly below what grade enrolment and repeater numbers suggest. It is also possible that the current system records some dropouts as repeaters. The underreporting of dropouts and possible exaggeration of repeaters may suggest that schools artificially maximize enrolment numbers to maximize their entitlement to school grants.

One in five schools surveyed by the QSD survey in 2014 had average primary repetition rates of less than 10 percent, and one in eight had less than 5 percent repetition. These schools deserve closer attention in order to identify factors underlying superior performance. Regression analysis of data relating to

170 sampled schools found that in standard 1, the availability of classrooms and of funding for non-salary related recurrent expenditure were both positively associated with the promotion rate. Buttressed by the results of the official impact evaluation of PSIP, this evidence suggests that school grants have induced positive changes in a minority of schools. However, an R^2 of 0.144 (table 3.3) means that only 14.4 percent of the variation in school performance, as measured by promotion rates, is explained by the level of input availability. The remainder of school performance is likely a function of the quality of teaching and other aspects of service delivery, which are the focus of the following chapter.

Notes

1. Report for Study on Student Repetition and Attrition in Primary Education in Malawi, USAID, September 2014.
2. Gross intake rate (GIR) is the proportion of all new entrants in standard 1 to the total number of 6-year-olds in the population, while the net intake rate (NIR) is the corresponding proportion with the number of new entrants who are 6 years old in the numerator.
3. Education Sector Implementation Plan II.

CHAPTER 4

Service Quality and Outcomes

Chapter 3 outlined how inputs per pupil—including teachers, textbooks and classrooms—account for less than 15 percent of the variation in the internal efficiency of primary schools, as measured by the rates of progression of pupils from one grade to the next. Much of the remaining variation is linked to the quality of services delivered using these inputs available. Moreover, a pupil's completion of the primary cycle is a necessary, but not sufficient, condition for achieving the desired goal of universal primary education. What students learn in school matters, and what students learn depends on teacher knowledge, teaching skills, and time spent in class.

This chapter focuses on (i) the quality of service delivery, (ii) learning outcomes, and (iii) the equity of these outcomes—the extent to which the benefits of primary education are distributed evenly among different income and gender groups. The quality of services delivered is examined by looking at: (i) what teachers know (teacher knowledge); (ii) how much they work (effort); and (iii) how teachers teach and how well they relate to students (practices and behavior). The objective of this chapter is to identify the factors that hinder and enable the effective delivery of teaching services in primary schools.

Teacher Knowledge

An analysis of evidence from two surveys conducted in 2011 and 2012 which tested teacher knowledge demonstrated that the majority of primary teachers were skilled in basic mathematics but not in its application to solve problems (table 4.1).

The SACMEQ II (2002) and SACMEQ III (2007) results showed that teachers in Malawi performed reasonably well on standard 6 tests in reading and mathematics, implying that they possessed sufficient knowledge to teach the primary grades 1 through 6. However, the results of these surveys found that Malawian teachers were not adequately knowledgeable to impart problem solving and critical reading skills to higher grade pupils in grades 7 and 8.

Table 4.1 Basic Mathematical Skills of Primary Teachers

Mean proportion of teachers who got it right	2011		2012	
Mathematics	Mean	Std. Dev	Mean	Std. Dev
Highest Common Factor	0.81	0.0098	0.82	0.01
Lowest Common Multiplier	0.75	0.011	0.75	0.011
Application of a Math function (Division)	0.77	0.0106	0.76	0.011
Application of a Math function (Percentage)	0.61	0.012	0.59	0.012
Decimals	0.76	0.0108	0.53	0.013
Interpreting simple graphs	0.65	0.012	0.95	0.005
Measurement of area of shapes 1	0.78	0.01	0.71	0.011
Measurement of area of shapes 2	0.5	0.012	0.53	0.013
Pedagogy (identifying mistakes and correcting it)	0.74	0.006	0.58	0.004

Sources: (i) Malawi Integrated Household Survey 2011; and (ii) Integrated Household Panel Survey 2013.

Teacher Effort

Teacher effort may be measured by (i) their presence in school; and (ii) time spent on tasks and activities in an average working day. Teacher absenteeism in Malawi, reported at an average of 15–20 days of instruction per teacher per academic year, at first glance appears to be relatively low (table 4.2). However, only 58 percent of schools observed by the QSD survey in 2014 maintained records on teacher absenteeism, and 17 percent of schools reported that teachers frequently absented themselves without prior permission or information.

In 2014, the average Malawian primary school teacher reported that they taught 33 periods in an average five-day working week. If one considers that the prescribed time for each period is 35 minutes, this means that the average teacher teaches for less than four hours per day.

A teacher who teaches less, and is absent more often than the average teacher, is less likely to accurately report contact time with students in classrooms. As a consequence, answers to survey questions relating to teacher effort need to be treated with caution. A curious outcome arising from analysis of the QSD survey data is that the amount of time teachers reported spending on "preparation for classes" is positively correlated with the repetition rate. The QSD survey collected data from 172 schools with regard to teacher time spent in the classroom and on class preparation as applicable to standard 5. In the 21 best performing schools (with less than 5 percent repetition rate), teachers of standard 5 reported spending on average 5.4 hours per week preparing for 33.1 teaching periods. In the remaining 151 schools with higher repetition rates, standard 5 teachers reported spending on average 12.4 hours per week preparing for approximately the same teaching load. The association between higher reported levels of class preparation time and a higher repetition rate is statistically significant (table 4.3), and supports the hypothesis that teachers who spend less time and effort in class tend to overreport the amount of time they spend preparing for class.

Table 4.2 Teacher Absenteeism in Primary Schools

	2011	2012	2014
Proportion of schools with teacher absence record	45%	69%	58%
Mean teacher absence full days in Term 2	41.8	39.6	58.5
Mean teacher absence partial days in Term 2	20.1	23.8	43.6
Mean full absence days per teacher in Term 2	3.9	3.0	9.0
Mean partial absence days per teacher in Term 2	1.9	1.8	1.0
Mean absence days per teacher in Term 2	5.8	4.8	9.8
Mean absence days per teacher in the whole academic year	17.3	14.5	20.3
Mean number of teachers per school	10.7	13.3	14.7
Proportion of schools with uninformed teacher absence	19%	19%	17%

Sources: School Surveys (WB 2011, 2012) and QSD Survey 2014.

Table 4.3 Negative Impact of Reported "Preparation Time"

	Repetition rate	
Characteristics of sample primary schools	<5%	>5%
Responses of Teachers of Grade 5		
Average periods of teaching per week	33.1	33.9
Average hours spent per week preparing for lessons	5.4***	12.4***
% of teachers in grade 5 with upper secondary level	90.5	87.4
Number of schools	**21**	**151**

Source: QSD Survey 2014.
Note: ***Significant at 99 percent confidence level.

An analysis of observed classroom activity (figure 4.1) shows that for approximately 20 percent of instructional time, teachers and students were off-task (no instructional activity was taking place due to the teacher being otherwise occupied or not being present in the classroom). Approximately 35 percent of each period was observed to be spent on passive learning, a context in which teachers provide information and passively students listen. In 20 percent of an average period of observed classroom instruction, students were engaged in rote learning, repeating verbally what is said by the teacher or copying notes from the blackboard. In the average observed instructional period, only 25 percent of time was dedicated to active teaching and learning activities, for example through discussions, group work, activities, answering questions, etc.

Chapter 2 described large variations in PTR across the lower and upper levels of primary education, with PTR above 100:1 in the lowest two grades and below 40:1 in the highest two grades. Teachers of standards 1 and 2 are generally overburdened, with one teacher per over-crowded section; while subject teachers in the upper primary grades have work schedules integrating considerable periods

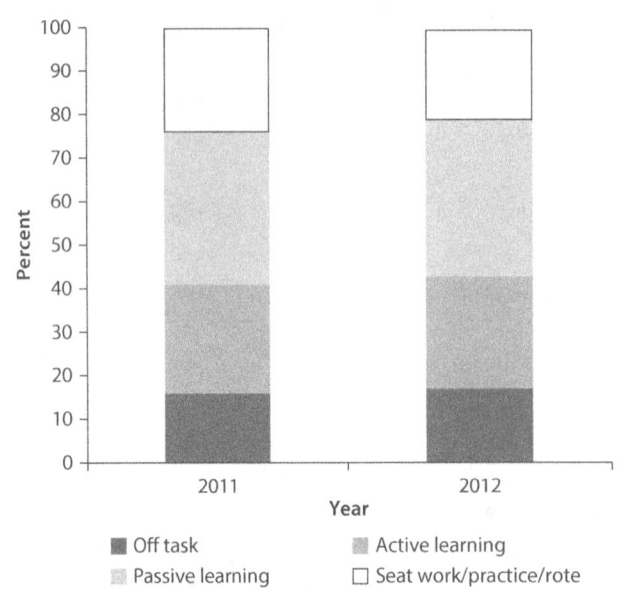

Figure 4.1 Time on Task in Classrooms

- Off task
- Active learning
- Passive learning
- Seat work/practice/rote

Sources: School Surveys (World Bank 2011, 2012).

of spare time. An optimal utilization of available teachers and a rational distribution of workload would require subject teachers to take on additional tasks to ease pressures at the lower level.

Teacher Practices and Behavior

The findings of the sample surveys reveal several encouraging facts about teacher practices, and some areas of concern. On the positive side, in more than 80 percent of observed cases, teachers had prepared a lesson plan for the session, and were regularly observed to ask questions of students to assess how much they had learnt. In the majority of observed class sessions, there was evidence of teachers giving positive feedback (encouragement and praise) to students. In approximately half of observed sessions, teachers were also observed scolding students for mistakes.

An area of concern arising from surveys is that in only 10 percent of cases students were observed to be asking questions of teachers for further clarification. Moreover, teachers appear to have become accustomed to teaching without requiring students to refer to textbooks, with textbooks only observed in use in half of observed classrooms, with more frequent use in standards 3 and 5 compared to standard 6. Chalkboards were observed to be used extensively, but in most cases only by the teacher. In the majority of observed classes, teachers copied their lessons, wrote questions and summarized take-away points on the chalkboard. In observed classrooms, approximately 80 percent of students had exercise books.

The USAID study identified types of teacher-student interaction contributing to poor school efficiency outcomes. Focus group discussions with members of School Management Committees and DEMs revealed that it was common for teachers to mock repeaters and overage girls, who in some instances are encouraged to leave school and get married. The study also revealed that some teachers enter into sexual relationships with overage girls, increasing the risk of early pregnancies and the spread of sexually transmitted diseases. Improper behavior and attitudes on the part of teachers leads to demoralization and frustration among students, and contributes to high levels of rates of absenteeism, repetition and dropout. Even in cases when improper teacher behavior is reported, this often only results in the offending teachers being transferred to another school, with little support given to victimized girls who are more likely to drop out of school as a consequence.

Teacher Incentives and Motivation

The Malawian primary education system is characterized by the general absence of mechanisms enabling an accurate assessment of teacher performance, and poor linkages between teacher performance and levels of remuneration and promotion.

The QSD survey found that 40 percent of interviewed teachers were happy with their work location. Of the sub-sample of teachers expressing contentedness with their place of work, 65 percent cited the proximity of their school to their home or village as the primary factor informing their assessment; 15 percent cited the proximity of a tarmac road or trading center to their school; and 8 percent cited the availability of teacher accommodation. Of the 60 percent of teachers who were not happy with their place of placement, approximately 50 percent cited long distances between their homes and place of work as the primary reason informing their assessment; 26 percent cited long distances from their place of work to a tarmac road or trading center; and 18 percent of dissatisfied teachers cited the absence of teacher accommodation at the school campus.

Feedback from teachers demonstrates a strong preference for placement in a school close to their home, and in the absence thereof, that teachers value the proximity of schools to transport infrastructure and amenities, as well as the presence of staff accommodation. This feedback bolsters the argument that teachers posted in the least attractive locations, where teacher shortages are generally most acute, should be adequately compensated for their relative hardship, and/or that the teacher deployment system should incorporate a rotation mechanisms wherein all teachers are required to serve in remote locations for selected periods in their career. The current system does incorporate a rural posting allowance which is meant to compensate rural teachers for their relative hardship, however this allowance is treated as an entitlement for all teachers posted in rural schools, and the provision thereof does not take into account the fact that not all rural schools are equally remote. Moreover, interviews with DEMs undertaken through the QSD survey revealed that not all eligible rural teachers actually receive their allowance. Teachers in schools closer to town are reportedly more likely to receive the allowance on a timely basis, while teachers in comparatively remote locations are less likely to receive the allowance. Poor coverage of the most remotely posted teachers, who are most in need of compensation for relative hardship, contributes to dissatisfaction and poor motivation on the part of teachers posted to remote and hard to reach places.

Learning Outcomes

The Malawi National Examinations Board (MANEB) was established in 1987 to carry out the Primary School Leaving Certificate Examinations (PSLCE), to certify that students had achieved the minimum levels of learning required for admission to the lower secondary level (standard 9). Results of the PSLCE administered in 2014 show that 69 percent of students who sat the exam obtained a passing grade. The 2014 results represent a marginal improvement on the 67.7 percent of students who passed in 2013 and 68.8 percent in 2011. However, results are not strictly comparable across years due to the fact that the PSLCE is not aligned with any fixed standard of competency.

There have been two attempts to assess primary learning achievement through standardized national assessments: (i) the Primary Achievement Sample Survey (PASS) conducted by MoEST with World Bank support and technical assistance in 2008; and (ii) the Monitoring Learning Achievement (MLA) administered with support from the United Nations Children's Fund (UNICEF) in 2012. The 2008 PASS study aimed to assess English and mathematics proficiency in grades 3, 5 and 7, while the 2012 MLA study assessed proficiency in the Chichewa language in addition to English and mathematics with a focus on pupils enrolled in grades 2, 4 and 7. The results of these assessments show that, in spite of an apparent improvement in pass rates as a proxy for student performance between 2008 and 2012 (table 4.4), the majority of those who passed in 2012 demonstrated only partial proficiency in mathematics by standard 7, with less than 10 percent of students surveyed demonstrating acceptable proficiency in mathematics (table 4.5).

The results of standardized international learning assessments administered under the auspices of SACMEQ show that Malawian pupils perform poorly with

Table 4.4 Pass Rates in Learning Assessments, 2008 and 2012

	2008 PASS Study (%)			2012 MLA study (%)		
Subject	Std-3	Std-5	Std-7	Std-2	Std-4	Std-7
English	10	11	12	22	18	24
Mathematics	20	10	11	40	55	37
Chichewa				16	30	40

Sources: (i) PASS conducted by MoEST in 2008; and (ii) MLA sponsored by UNICEF in 2012.

Table 4.5 Distribution of Pupils by Proficiency Level in Mathematics in 2012 (percentage)

Level of achievement	Std-2 (%)	Std-4 (%)	Std-7(%)
Level 1 (no achievement)	49	23	59
Level 2 (partial achievement)	24	31	35
Level 3 (acceptable achievement)	22	34	2
Level 4 (excellent achievement)	5	12	4

Source: Monitoring Learning Achievement (MLA) in 2012, supported by UNICEF.

Table 4.6 Mean Scores in International Learning Assessments

	Reading (SE)	Mathematics (SE)
SACMEQ II (2002)	428.9 (2.37)	432.9 (2.24)
SACMEQ III (2007)	433.5 (2.63)	447.0 (2.89)

Source: Southern & Eastern African Consortium for Monitoring Education Quality.
Note: Figures in parenthesis indicate standard errors of estimation.

regard to proficiency in both reading and mathematics. While mean Malawian scores increased slightly between 2002 and 2007 (table 4.6), they were still lower than 500, the average for all SACMEQ countries.

Equity of Outcomes

Children from the poorest 20 percent of households account for 29 percent of enrolment in public primary schools, and 17 percent in private schools. By comparison, children from the richest households constitute 10 percent of enrolment in public schools and 24 percent of private primary school enrolment. Enrolment of children in public primary schools consistently declines as household income increases, regardless of the gender of the child or region of residence. In other words, the distribution of benefits associated with public expenditure on primary education is progressive, and is more than proportionately targeted at the poor.

The progressive profile of spending on public primary education is unique in comparison with all other subsectors of the education system. In higher levels of Malawian public education the benefit incidence is regressive, meaning that public spending is more than proportionately targeted at richer citizens. In primary education, the poorest quintile (20 percent of population) receives 29 percent, the largest share, of government subsidy, while the share of the subsidy for the richest quintile of the population is only 9 percent. In secondary education, the share of the government subsidy accruing to the poorest quintile of the population is only 10 percent compared to 28 percent for the richest quintile. The regressive incidence of benefits is most pronounced at the tertiary level, where the poorest quintile of the population receives only 1 percent of the government subsidy compared to 82 percent for the richest quintile.[1]

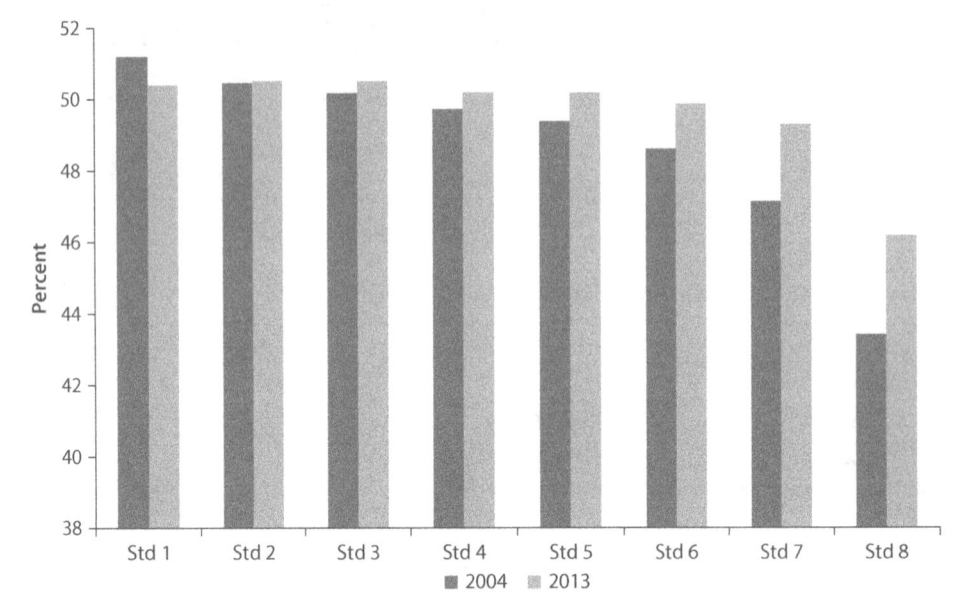

Figure 4.2 Proportion of Girls in Primary Enrollment

[Bar chart showing percent of girls enrolled by standard (Std 1–Std 8) for years 2004 and 2013. Y-axis: Percent, ranging from 38 to 52.]

Source: Annex Table A3.1 (a) and A3.1 (b) of this report.

In the early grades of primary education male and female students are represented in approximately equal numbers. In standards 7 and 8 the effects of higher dropout rates among girls are evident, and the proportion of female students falls below 50 percent (figure 4.2). The burden of inadequate school infrastructure—for example the absence of adequate toilet facilities—falls disproportionately on girls. Poor water and sanitation facilities present over-age girls in primary classes with unique challenges during menstruation, leading to high rates of absenteeism. These, and other, factors negatively influence learning among girls, leading to generally higher levels of repetition and dropout among female students.

The interaction of inadequate classroom furniture and cultural biases also contributes to the perpetuation of gender discrimination: In situations where there are insufficient chairs to accommodate all students, boys are given privileged access to chairs and girls are required to squat on the floor. Schools could be advised to allocate and use available furniture in ways as to ensure that either all students in a class sit on chairs or all of them sit on the floor.

Summary of Conclusions

Effort and motivation on the part of teachers, and the quality of teaching, critically impact primary school completion rates and learning achievement. Improving the performance and educational outcomes of primary schools in Malawi depends less on increasing the supply of teachers than on improving the work practices of existing teachers.

Teachers at the lowest grades are relatively over-burdened compared to those teaching upper primary grades, many of whom are subject specialist teachers with significant stocks of unused time. Optimizing the utilization of available teachers is to a large extent the responsibility of the Head Teachers and school management committees who are collectively responsible for developing SIPs, a precondition for accessing school grants. Head teacher training needs to incorporate new content to encourage innovation in leading interventions to improve learning outcomes and the optimization of available resources in the lower primary grades.

In addition to school level initiatives, there is considerable scope for MoEST to identify and implement programs improving the distribution of teachers across schools, as shown in chapter 2, as well as across districts, as discussed in this chapter. There is also an urgent need to address challenges faced by approximately half of all primary school teachers with regard to the remoteness of school locations, the absence of housing alternatives closer to school sites, and to optimize the distribution of rural posting allowances to ensure that teachers in remote schools receive adequate compensation.

There is a strong case to be made for increasing the share of public education expenditure accruing to basic education on the basis of equity, due to the fact that public spending on primary education more effectively targets poor households than other sub-sector. Moreover, pedagogical weaknesses evident in the foundational lower primary grades will require special attention. For practical reasons, it makes sense to deepen the devolution of funding and decision-making to the school level. However, enhancing funding of schools through SIGs will require the weighing of design considerations to ensure that funding is sufficiently aligned to promote intended outcomes and that monies provided through SIGs do not generate adverse incentives.

Note

1. Malawi Public Expenditure Review, The World Bank, 2013.

CHAPTER 5

Reform Program and Financing Strategy

This chapter will commence with an assessment of the government's own diagnosis of challenges in the primary education sub-sector, a contingent assessment of the reform program intended to address them, and thereafter propose ways in which the government's program may be strengthened to enhance the likelihood of success. This chapter will examine the financing strategy presented in ESIP-II, to assess the extent to which the allocation of limited resources is practically aligned with the priorities of the sector plan. Suggestions will be made with regard to ways in which the financing strategy could be improved to enhance the likelihood of the ESIP-II meeting its goals for basic education in Malawi. The final section of the chapter presents a summary of the conclusions and key recommendations.

Government's Program and Financing Plan

MoEST recently published its ESIP-II to guide activities for the period 2013–18. The ESIP-II recognizes many of the challenges undermining the effective delivery of quality primary education in Malawi, including high rates of repetition, low output efficiency, poor learning outcomes and gender disparities evident in rates of student survival and completion. The ESIP-II presents a reform program to address these problems and projects three alternative financing scenarios.

"To ensure that 50 percent of children reach Standard 4 literacy and numeracy levels by 2017" is defined as the immediate goal for basic education, to be achieved through the following measures:

- The lengthening of the school day from three to four hours daily for lower standards, and the promotion of a greater focus on "early grade" reading and mathematics
- Ensuring the improved availability of textbooks at the start of the school year by devolving textbook procurement to the schools
- The construction of 1,500 additional classrooms each year, to support the achievement of a PTR of 90:1 by 2017/18, with priority given to classroom construction in support of lower standards

- A comprehensive strategy to improve teacher motivation, including more comprehensive and transparent mechanisms for teacher promotion and clearer disciplinary measures, especially with regard to teacher attendance
- The imposition of a mandated cap on repetition of 10 percent per class
- Support for remedial teaching and
- The strengthening of school-based management as the foundation of ESIP II, to be achieved through additional funding for PSIP, including school grants.

Given considerable uncertainty regarding future levels of external donor support for the education sector, ESIP-II presents three education financing scenarios for the 2013–18 period, corresponding with "low," "medium" and "high" levels of donor assistance, with expenditure for each education sub-sector and major components tailored in line with the three scenarios.

In 2013/14 on-budget external donor support for education in Malawi was MK 36.13 billion. Under the "high" funding scenario, on-budget external donor support for education is projected to reach MK 46.17bn in 2017/18, declining to MK 29.19bn under the "medium" scenario, and MK 19.49bn under the "low" scenario (table 5.1).

The high funding scenario models resource allocation based on a situation in which donors resume previous levels of support for both the pooled financing mechanism (SWAp) and through discrete projects. The medium funding scenario assumes that pooled financing will decline and stay at a low level, while project-specific funding will be restored. The low funding scenario is based on assumptions premised on low levels of support for the pooled funding mechanisms, and discrete projects. The medium funding scenario most closely approximates the

Table 5.1 Education Resource Envelope—Alternative Scenarios, 2013–18

MK billion	2013/14	2014/15	2015/16	2016/17	2017/18
High Funding Scenario					
Total Education Funding (on-budget)	**98.52**	**120.11**	**131.64**	**149.63**	**165.13**
Domestic Financing	62.40	78.97	85.95	100.80	118.96
External Donor Financing	36.13	41.14	45.70	48.84	46.17
Medium Funding Scenario					
Total Education Funding (on-budget)	**98.52**	**102.29**	**112.05**	**128.75**	**146.00**
Domestic Financing	62.40	78.79	93.25	101.51	116.81
External Donor Financing	36.13	23.50	18.80	27.24	29.19
Low Funding Scenario					
Total Education Funding (on-budget)	**98.52**	**97.32**	**109.08**	**120.68**	**134.77**
Domestic Financing	62.40	81.21	100.76	102.62	115.29
External Donor Financing	36.13	16.11	8.33	18.06	19.49

Source: Education Sector Development Plan (ESIP II).

present situation, and should be considered a "base case scenario" for the purposes of analysis.

The composition of on-budget education expenditure is projected to favor an increased allocation for primary education under all three scenarios (table 5.2).

Table 5.2 Projected Composition of Education Expenditure, 2013–18

MK billion	2013/14	2014/15	2015/16	2016/17	2017/18
High Funding Scenario					
Primary Education	44.4%	50.1%	49.8%	51.0%	52.3%
Primary Teacher Training	6.3%	3.3%	3.0%	2.7%	2.3%
Other Basic Education	1.5%	1.2%	1.1%	1.0%	0.9%
Secondary Education	13.3%	15.6%	18.7%	19.3%	19.9%
Secondary Teacher Training	1.3%	1.2%	1.1%	1.0%	1.0%
Higher Education	30.1%	25.2%	23.3%	22.1%	20.9%
Technical & Vocational (TEVET)	0.5%	0.5%	0.5%	0.5%	0.5%
Administration & Support	2.7%	2.8%	2.6%	2.4%	2.3%
Education Exp (on-budget)	100.0%	100.0%	100.0%	100.0%	100.0%
Medium Funding Scenario					
Primary Education	44.4%	50.2%	50.3%	51.6%	53.1%
Primary Teacher Training	6.3%	2.8%	2.5%	2.3%	2.0%
Other Basic Education	1.5%	0.9%	0.8%	0.7%	0.7%
Secondary Education	13.3%	15.7%	18.3%	18.7%	19.2%
Secondary Teacher Training	1.3%	0.9%	0.8%	0.7%	0.7%
Higher Education	30.1%	25.8%	24.0%	22.7%	21.4%
Technical & Vocational (TEVET)	0.5%	0.5%	0.5%	0.5%	0.5%
Administration & Support	2.7%	3.1%	2.8%	2.7%	2.5%
Education Exp (on-budget)	100.0%	100.0%	100.0%	100.0%	100.0%
Low Funding Scenario					
Primary Education	44.4%	50.4%	50.9%	52.4%	54.0%
Primary Teacher Training	6.3%	2.2%	2.0%	1.8%	1.6%
Other Basic Education	1.5%	0.5%	0.4%	0.4%	0.4%
Secondary Education	13.3%	15.9%	17.8%	17.9%	18.2%
Secondary Teacher Training	1.3%	0.5%	0.5%	0.4%	0.4%
Higher Education	30.1%	26.4%	24.7%	23.5%	22.1%
Technical & Vocational (TEVET)	0.5%	0.6%	0.6%	0.6%	0.6%
Administration & Support	2.7%	3.5%	3.2%	3.0%	2.8%
Education Exp (on-budget)	100.0%	100.0%	100.0%	100.0%	100.0%
Memo Item: Share of Salary Bill					
High Funding Scenario	44.9%	46.7%	47.3%	49.4%	51.7%
Medium Funding Scenario	44.9%	52.1%	53.0%	55.2%	57.5%
Low Funding Scenario	44.9%	57.6%	58.7%	61.1%	63.3%

Source: ESIP-II.

The share of expenditure on primary education and primary teacher training, taken together, is projected to rise from 50.1 percent in 2013/14 to 55.1 percent in 2017/18 under the medium funding (base case) scenario. The share of expenditure allocated to secondary education is also projected to rise, while the share accruing to higher education is projected to decline considerably. These trends are broadly aligned with the government's policy intended to strengthen the base of the education sector (lower primary level, basic literacy and numeracy skills), build capacity at secondary level, and gradually reduce the level of government subsidy for students at the tertiary level.

Critical Appraisal

The financing scenarios included in the ESIP-II do not include off-budget funding of basic education. As a result of this omission, the plan frames the annual target of 1,500 additional classrooms for lower primary grades as an "aspiration" as opposed to a firm target with dedicated financing. Given that a shortage of classroom space is one of the most binding constraints affecting primary school performance, the omission of off-budget funding for basic education represents a serious weakness in the presented financial projections.

An appraisal of ESIP-II, conducted on behalf of external development partners and domestic non-governmental agencies, noted that the plan represents a *"revolutionary shift of emphasis"* toward the first four grades of primary education and toward a focus on basic literacy and numeracy skills. The appraisal, however, cautioned that *"there remains a good deal of work [to be done] to translate the excellent priorities [articulated in ESP-II] into a multi-year implementation plan."*[1] Analysis presented in this report suggests that the GoM's reform program is correctly orientated from a policy perspective, but that envisaged interventions will not be sufficient to address deep-rooted and systemic problems. Moreover, the allocation of financial resources is not fully aligned with the policy priorities and targets of the ESP-II.

To translate prioritized targets into a credible action plan, it is necessary to find ways to catalyze change in the primary school system to improve its overall performance. A silver lining in this regard is the presence of some schools within the existing system that have improved performance through effective use of school grants. A key for motivating system-wide change will be the identification of factors informing success in better performing schools, and the use of this evidence to generalize success across the system. In this regard, it will be worth investing in (i) further research to identify performance features of the most successful schools, i.e., schools with significantly lower than average rates of repetition and higher rates of promotion and learning achievement; and (ii) an effective communication campaign to publicize the successes of these schools, to encourage others to emulate them.

School Grant Reform

ESIP-II articulates the need to improve the alignment of school funding with needs through the reform of aspects of the formula for determining school grants. The analysis presented in chapter 3 suggests that there is need to think more deeply about school grant reform, with a close focus on the incentives generated. The most critical change in this regard is to break the link between grant entitlement and student enrolment. The current formula generates perverse incentives for schools to maintain pupils who have virtually dropped out of the system on school rolls, and skews the attention of schools toward maximizing enrolment and away from improving the number of students who complete a full cycle of primary education with the desired levels of numeracy and literacy skills.

An option that should be considered to more effectively orientate the allocation of SIGs with objectives to improve educational outcomes would be to replace measures of enrolment with determinants of "effective pupil years" in the formulation of school grants. This is likely to be more effective in bringing down repetition rates than the approach proposed in the ESIP-II to impose a cap of 10 percent on the proportion of repeating students in any primary grade. Caps have been imposed in the past with little tangible impact on the ground. Changes to the formula for the determination of SIGs should be introduced over a period of two years, to more effectively align school grant entitlement with improvements to learning outcomes, and to encourage the generalization of best practices evident in outlier, high performing schools, across the system as a whole.

Expenditure Composition and Input Mix

A highly concerning feature of the ESIP-II is that the share of expenditure in the education budget dedicated to the servicing of the salary bill is projected to rise in all three scenarios. Even under the scenario modeling high levels of support from external donors, the share of resources allocated to recurrent personnel emoluments (PE) is projected to rise from 44.9 percent of total expenditure to 51.7 percent over four years.

The share of recurrent personnel expenditure in primary education is much higher than for the sector as a whole, constituting 84 percent of total expenditure in 2013/14 (table 2.3 in chapter 2). The share of resources dedicated to servicing salaries and associated supplements significantly limits space for the financing of essential non-salary related recurrent and capital expenditure. In a context wherein shortages of classroom infrastructure and learning materials have more of a negative impact on learning outcomes than the shortage of teachers, a further rise in the share of expenditure dedicated to salaries represents the further misalignment of resources with needs.

In light of existing levels of expenditure on salaries, it will be important to focus on measures to generate additional teaching time at low cost through improving the allocation of available teacher capacity. In this context, the government should limit the hiring of additional teachers to prevent a further increase in the share of recurrent expenditure dedicated to salaries, and to create fiscal space for expenditure on non-salary related inputs.

A more gradual approach to the hiring of additional primary school teachers, in conjunction with the introduction of measures to constrain salary adjustments (such as aligning upward adjustments to salaries with consumer inflation for three years), the introduction of stricter controls to ensure transparency and accountability in the provision of allowances, and the rationalization thereof, would free up resources to support expenditure on critical non-staff inputs including classrooms, infrastructure maintenance, workbooks, textbooks, etc.

A key conclusion of the recent official impact evaluation of the PSIP—validated by the findings of this report—is the recognition of the critical role non-staff inputs, acquired by schools under PSIP, play in improving the internal efficiency of primary schools (through reducing repetition and dropouts). However, the financing plan for the ESIP-II makes the scaling-up of PSIP grants contingent on the availability of external donor funding. The ESIP-II explicitly states that *"Resources permitting, funding for PSIP is scaled upwards..."*[2] An over-dependence on foreign donors to support the expansion of PSIP is the result of the disproportionate share of public resources accruing in support of the existing salary bill.

In addition to addressing escalating salary-related expenditure, serious attention must be paid to the funding of allowances. The 2013 Public Expenditure Review highlighted significant potential savings that could be achieved through the introduction of stricter controls over travel related allowances to civil servants, including teachers. The findings presented in this report underscore the need to rationalize allowances for primary teachers to more effectively align their provision with efforts to improve teacher motivation, such as the targeting of rural allowances to teachers posted in the most remote and hard-to-reach locations.

Teacher Management

The ESIP-II recognizes problems associated with low levels of teacher motivation and the low number of hours, on average, dedicated to teaching in a typical working day. The ESIP-II proposes the extension of the school day by one hour daily for lower grades (standards 1 to 4), and the introduction of more transparent mechanisms for the promotion of teachers. While these proposed interventions are perhaps necessary, they are insufficient to holistically address problems associated with low teacher effort and motivation.

Problems associated with inadequate effort, and the low number of hours dedicated to teaching, are not experienced uniformly across the primary subsector. In the lowest grades, teachers typically struggle to manage large classes in overcrowded classrooms, or must teach 80–100 pupils outdoors. Teachers in standards 4 to 8 typically have a much lower teaching burden due to smaller class sizes, and due to the fact that subject specialist teachers enjoy considerable spare time during school hours. Extending school hours by an hour for the lower grades will not address problems associated with the inequitable distribution of teaching workloads, and further interventions will be required to mandate and/or incentivize teachers of standards 4 to 8 to contribute to the alleviation of teaching burdens in the lower grades.

In order to address problems associated with poor teacher motivation in remote and hard-to-reach locations, it will be necessary to address the anomalies and inequities present in the existing system of allowances for rural teachers. Evidence suggests that rural teachers with relatively good access to urban centers may draw a disproportionate share of rural allowances. In the short term, an in-depth review of the provision and distribution of rural allowances is required to inform the design and implementation of interventions to optimize the use of allowances to recognize and reward teachers working in the most difficult and remote conditions. Over the medium term, there is a need to review and rationalize all teacher allowances, to optimize their targeting and effectiveness for improving the motivation of teachers, in addition to the introduction of performance-based promotion policies.

Reform of Textbook Supply

The ESIP-II recognizes problems associated with the current system of centralized procurement associated with the delays in the supply and underutilization of textbooks. In order to alleviate these problems, the ESIP-II proposes the devolution of textbook procurement to schools which will commence through a pilot project. The relative success of a devolved system of textbook procurement will depend to a large extent on (i) the capacity of schools to oversee and manage textbook procurement; and (ii) the availability of textbooks in local markets. Currently, both of these conditions are largely absent or unknown. In this context it would be wise to develop alternative options to be piloted in conjunction with the current ESIP-II proposal, before making a decision with regard to the scaling-up of the most effective mix of interventions. An alternative that should be considered could utilize a public–private approach for promoting the development of local markets in which students can purchase textbooks so that they can take them home and use them in their spare time. This could be supplemented by a textbook grant, to be incorporated through SIGs, to be used to ensure that poor students are able to afford textbooks. Such a policy would improve textbook utilization, improve cost recovery and reduce net expenditure on textbooks. In the short to medium term this model would moreover encourage the development of a second-hand market for textbooks that, over time, would reduce overall costs to government and households.

Financing Classroom Construction

The provision of additional classroom space has the most verifiable impact on student survival and completion in primary schools in Malawi. Insufficient classroom space is among the most binding constraints hindering improved performance of the primary sub-sector. ESIP-II sets an aspirational goal for the creation of 1,500 additional classrooms per year, but does not clearly identify how the achievement of this relatively modest target would be financed.

The expansion of the stock of classroom infrastructure is an area in which external donor support can be mobilized and channeled through ring-fenced financing mechanisms. Moreover, support for classroom construction could be targeted toward schools in the top quartile of pupils-per-classroom ratios that have shown signs of improved performance.

In light of existing resource constraints facing the education sector in Malawi, MoEST would benefit from integrating all available resources into one financing plan. At present, off-budget donor projects are not fully integrated into existing systems, undermining holistic planning processes. Overall financial management of the sector would benefit from the introduction of an integrated accounting framework inclusive of all external donor support detailing the composition of off-budget expenditure.

Conclusions

The GoM's current education sector plan is appropriately focused on improving service delivery in the lowest grades of primary education. However, the proposed agenda for reform is not extensive enough to address systemic constraints, and resource allocation is insufficiently aligned with targeted priorities. The current plan for the financing of reforms, moreover, may serve to undermine ongoing dialogue between the government and its development partners. Development partners have articulated improved educational outcomes as a conditional requirement for additional support, while the government's plan outlines scenarios in which additional donor support is a precondition for improved performance and outcomes.

A more credible approach, with a greater chance of restoring donor confidence and encouraging fruitful donor–government partnership, would be a commitment on the part of the GoM, using only domestic resources and existing external support, to protect and enhance the share of non-salary expenditure in general, and to strengthen PSIP grants in particular. In this context, development partners could be invited to "top up" programs through targeted support to schools demonstrating improved performance.

Given a constrained resource envelope for education, and uncertainty with regard to external support for the sector going forward, it would be prudent to align the financing plan of the ESP-II with the base case scenario articulated under the "medium" support scenario of the current plan. In order to accommodate potential changes in the funding environment, the base case scenario could be accompanied by a contingency plan framing guidelines to be implemented to adjust overall financing for both upside and downside variations in funding.

Contingency planning should take into account the possibility for variation not only in external donor support but also in the availability of domestic resources due to fluctuations in economic growth and the outcomes of ongoing tax reform initiatives. In the event that additional domestic resources become available, expenditure could be used to finance increased teacher recruitment. In a context of additional external off-budget or ring-fenced on-budget project support, additional resources could be dedicated to the creation of more classroom space and the further strengthening of quality and learning outcomes in primary schools through a top-up component to the school grants program targeting schools demonstrating improved performance.

Note

1. HEART Report on Appraisal of ESIP-II, commissioned by DFID on behalf of Development Partners and Local Education Group in Malawi.
2. ESIP-II.

APPENDIX A

Tables

Table A2.1 (a) Sources and Uses of Funds in Education, 2011/12

K billions	2011/12			
	Approved Budget	Revised Budget	Actual Outturn	Execution rate (%)
Sources/Channels of Funds:				
Recurrent Funding on Budget	**46.45**	**53.47**	**53.40**	**99.9**
MoEST—Salary Bill	27.48	27.48	28.23	*102.7*
MoEST—Other Recurrent Transactions (ORT)	3.81	10.08	9.48	*94.0*
Local Councils (ORT)	3.42	4.16	3.41	*81.9*
Subventions (ORT)	11.74	11.74	12.28	*104.6*
Development Funding on Budget	**6.54**	**10.09**	**7.87**	**77.9**
MoEST Development Projects	5.89	5.94	2.83	*47.6*
Local Development Fund (LDF)	0.00	3.51	3.51	*100.0*
Externally Funded Projects	0.65	0.65	1.53	*235.9*
Total	**52.99**	**63.56**	**61.26**	**96.4**
Uses of Funds:				
Primary Education (recurrent):	**23.37**	**27.24**	**24.40**	**89.6**
Salaries of Teachers and others	19.95	19.95	19.94	*100.0*
Material Supply through HQ	0.00	3.13	1.57	*50.0*
Non-salary recurrent costs at districts	3.42	4.16	2.90	*69.6*
Secondary (recurrent)	6.06	6.80	6.45	*94.9*
Tertiary and vocational (recurrent)	12.14	12.50	13.01	*104.1*
Teacher training (recurrent)	2.21	3.49	3.54	*101.4*
Management (recurrent):	0.46	1.23	4.61	*374.7*
Other Recurrent	0.00	0.00	1.38	
Total Recurrent Expenditure	46.45	51.26	53.40	*104.2*
Development Expenditure	6.54	10.09	7.87	*77.9*
Total	**52.99**	**61.36**	**61.26**	**99.8**

Source: Annual and Quarterly Financial Reports (from IFMIS), Finance Dept., MoEST.

Table A2.1 (b) Sources and Uses of Funds in Education, 2012/13

K billions	2012/13			
	Approved Budget	Revised Budget	Actual Outturn	Execution rate (%)
Sources/Channels of Funds:				
Recurrent funding on Budget	**64.41**	**76.68**	**76.98**	*100.4*
MoEST—Salary Bill	32.65	37.89	38.75	*102.3*
MoEST—Other Recurrent Transactions (ORT)	12.54	14.64	14.97	*102.3*
Local Councils (ORT)	5.69	5.77	4.87	*84.4*
Subventions (ORT)	13.53	18.38	18.38	*100.0*
Development Funding on Budget	**11.50**	**11.50**	**8.89**	*77.3*
MoEST Development Projects	5.13	5.13	3.25	*63.5*
Local Development Fund (LDF)	2.00	2.00	4.52	*226.1*
Externally Funded Projects	4.37	4.37	1.11	*25.5*
Total	**75.91**	**88.17**	**85.86**	*97.4*
Uses of Funds:				
Primary Education (recurrent):	**32.10**	**38.07**	**38.47**	*101.1*
Salaries of Teachers and others	24.74	29.04	29.45	*101.4*
Material Supply through HQ	1.67	3.26	3.81	*117.1*
Non-salary recurrent costs at districts	5.69	5.77	5.21	*90.2*
Secondary (recurrent)	9.94	10.58	9.10	*86.0*
Tertiary and vocational (recurrent)	14.46	19.33	19.31	*99.9*
Teacher training (recurrent)	5.94	6.29	6.03	*95.9*
Management (recurrent)	1.36	1.82	2.07	*113.9*
Other Recurrent	0.60	0.60	1.99	*331.2*
Total Recurrent Expenditure	64.41	76.68	76.98	*100.4*
Development Expenditure	11.50	11.50	8.89	*77.3*
Total	**75.91**	**88.17**	**85.86**	*97.4*

Source: Annual and Quarterly Financial Reports (from IFMIS), Finance Dept., MoEST.

Table A2.1 (c) Sources and Uses of Funds in Education, 2013/14

K billions	2013/14			
	Approved Budget	Revised Budget	Actual Outturn	Execution rate (%)
Sources/Channels of Funds:				
Recurrent Funding on Budget	**90.05**	**101.76**	**86.47**	*0.85*
MoEST—Salary Bill	44.69	56.40	52.75	*0.94*
MoEST—Other Recurrent Transactions (ORT)	12.82	12.82	12.28	*0.96*
Local Councils (ORT)	8.13	8.13	7.28	*0.89*
Subventions (ORT)	24.41	24.41	14.16	*0.58*

table continues next page

Table A2.1 (c)   Sources and Uses of Funds in Education, 2013/14 *(continued)*

K billions	2013/14			
	Approved Budget	Revised Budget	Actual Outturn	Execution rate (%)
Development Funding on Budget	**20.12**	**20.12**	**6.00**	**0.30**
MoEST Development Projects	9.78	9.78	2.70	0.28
Local Development Fund (LDF)	5.88	5.88	1.71	0.29
Externally Funded Projects	4.45	4.45	1.58	0.36
Total	**110.17**	**121.88**	**92.47**	**0.76**
Uses of Funds:				
Primary Education (recurrent):	**45.20**	**45.20**	**42.08**	**0.93**
Salaries of Teachers and others	35.40	35.40	35.19	0.99
Material Supply through HQ	1.67	1.67	1.55	0.93
Non-salary recurrent costs at districts	8.13	8.13	5.34	0.66
Secondary (recurrent)	11.50	11.50	7.70	0.67
Tertiary and vocational (recurrent)	23.15	25.17	14.32	0.57
Teacher training (recurrent)	6.20	6.27	5.12	0.82
Management (recurrent):	1.31	13.02	13.02	1.00
Other Recurrent	2.69	0.60	4.23	
Total Recurrent Expenditure	90.05	101.76	86.47	0.85
Development Expenditure	20.12	20.12	6.00	0.30
Total	**110.17**	**121.88**	**92.47**	**0.76**

Source: Annual and Quarterly Financial Reports (from IFMIS), Finance Dept., MoEST.

Table A3.1 (a)   Enrollment in Primary—Girls (Standard 1 to Standard 8), 2004/05 to 2013/14

(Number)	Std 1	Std 2	Std 3	Std 4	Std 5	Std 6	Std 7	Std 8	Primary
2004	447,073	286,496	252,501	184,528	148,097	110,140	83,822	63,936	1,576,593
2005	439,336	289,939	258,038	188,008	152,109	113,383	86,703	66,042	1,593,558
2006	452,390	290,633	265,932	194,618	158,532	118,532	91,348	69,845	1,641,830
2007	431,893	296,167	267,382	200,114	164,991	123,932	95,060	73,493	1,653,032
2008	444,623	333,669	293,981	218,375	178,792	136,667	105,190	83,186	1,794,483
2009	443,656	331,562	312,926	227,373	182,621	143,288	113,015	87,576	1,842,017
2010	459,103	342,111	319,785	253,544	197,398	151,843	124,076	95,064	1,942,924
2011	471,863	355,683	329,572	265,891	214,531	163,207	131,640	101,324	2,033,711
2012	486,976	364,432	335,080	274,745	225,306	173,420	136,528	103,547	2,100,034
2013	519,520	388,011	356,149	291,753	243,643	189,743	149,842	111,756	2,250,417

Source: EMIS 2004/05–2013/14.

Table A3.1 (b) Enrollment in Primary—Boys (Standard 1 to Standard 8), 2004/05 to 2013/14

(Number)	Std 1	Std 2	Std 3	Std 4	Std 5	Std 6	Std 7	Std 8	Primary
2004	425,993	281,247	250,735	186,598	151,776	116,456	94,013	83,375	1,590,193
2005	424,428	283,437	258,571	188,396	153,925	118,423	95,194	84,714	1,607,088
2006	434,122	284,067	264,018	193,522	157,064	120,265	97,479	88,347	1,638,884
2007	415,041	289,431	266,073	199,206	164,447	124,571	102,448	92,677	1,653,894
2008	435,794	329,288	295,117	216,921	176,684	138,017	110,679	103,788	1,806,288
2009	430,475	323,947	308,966	226,444	177,647	141,199	114,844	105,942	1,829,464
2010	446,058	338,664	314,773	250,595	194,157	149,372	125,128	106,972	1,925,719
2011	453,589	341,956	323,034	261,747	211,607	161,519	131,384	115,673	2,000,509
2012	473,150	354,819	331,803	269,825	223,275	174,794	140,376	120,851	2,088,893
2013	511,314	380,160	349,046	289,578	241,898	190,796	154,136	130,260	2,247,188

Source: EMIS 2004/05–2013/14.

Table A3.1 (c) Enrollment in Primary (Standard 1 to Standard 8), 2004/05 to 2013/14

(Number)	Std 1	Std 2	Std 3	Std 4	Std 5	Std 6	Std 7	Std 8	Primary
2004	873,066	567,743	503,236	371,126	299,873	226,596	177,835	147,311	3,166,786
2005	863,764	573,376	516,609	376,404	306,034	231,806	181,897	150,756	3,200,646
2006	886,512	574,700	529,950	388,140	315,596	238,797	188,827	158,192	3,280,714
2007	846,934	585,598	533,455	399,320	329,438	248,503	197,508	166,170	3,306,926
2008	880,417	662,957	589,098	435,296	355,476	274,684	215,869	186,974	3,600,771
2009	874,131	655,509	621,892	453,817	360,268	284,487	227,859	193,518	3,671,481
2010	905,161	680,775	634,558	504,139	391,555	301,215	249,204	202,036	3,868,643
2011	925,452	697,639	652,606	527,638	426,138	324,726	263,024	216,997	4,034,220
2012	960,126	719,251	666,883	544,570	448,581	348,214	276,904	224,398	4,188,927
2013	1,030,834	768,171	705,195	581,331	485,541	380,539	303,978	242,016	4,497,605

Source: EMIS 2004/05–2013/14.

Table A3.2 (a) Repeaters in Primary—Girls (Standard 1 to Standard 8), 2004/05 to 2013/14

(Number)	Std 1	Std 2	Std 3	Std 4	Std 5	Std 6	Std 7	Std 8	Total
2004	105,470	54,362	52,384	29,743	21,492	13,092	8,597	7,964	293,104
2005	106,291	60,657	52,558	29,757	21,942	13,280	8,999	8,755	302,239
2006	111,570	61,377	57,670	31,740	24,529	15,241	10,156	9,564	321,847
2007	104,817	62,088	59,252	33,302	25,913	15,481	10,620	10,682	322,155
2008	106,909	65,699	62,404	35,673	27,540	17,140	12,223	12,902	340,490
2009	100,701	63,660	60,719	34,515	24,470	15,398	11,769	13,207	324,439
2010	106,767	66,134	65,890	39,606	28,697	19,371	14,418	13,013	353,896
2011	110,973	69,978	66,959	44,961	32,911	22,345	17,433	16,800	382,360
2012	107,535	78,391	68,904	47,072	36,553	24,013	19,065	18,409	399,942
2013	117,395	72,287	66,210	47,817	37,819	26,544	21,325	19,809	409,206

Source: EMIS 2004/05–2013/14.

Table A3.2 (b) Repeaters in Primary—Boys (Standard 1 to Standard 8), 2004/05 to 2013/14

(Number)	Std 1	Std 2	Std 3	Std 4	Std 5	Std 6	Std 7	Std 8	Total
2004	101,486	55,997	54,604	31,494	22,785	14,239	9,288	12,149	302,042
2005	109,480	57,733	56,813	31,676	23,365	14,569	9,591	12,311	315,538
2006	110,720	62,328	59,094	33,545	25,826	15,675	10,729	13,819	331,736
2007	102,968	63,497	62,322	35,574	26,962	16,448	11,271	15,217	334,259
2008	107,918	67,318	66,610	38,892	28,347	17,492	12,794	18,344	357,715
2009	99,924	64,316	64,307	36,373	25,516	16,275	11,636	17,459	335,806
2010	107,816	66,424	65,915	40,403	29,717	19,893	14,866	16,291	361,325
2011	108,926	70,094	68,454	46,698	33,671	23,227	17,951	20,859	389,880
2012	107,442	72,586	71,891	49,049	37,620	24,633	19,316	22,189	404,726
2013	119,230	74,457	69,495	48,366	39,506	27,048	21,593	23,995	423,690

Source: EMIS 2004/05–2013/14.

Table A3.2 (c) Repeaters in Primary (Standard 1 to Standard 8), 2004/05 to 2013/14

(Number)	Std 1	Std 2	Std 3	Std 4	Std 5	Std 6	Std 7	Std 8	Total
2004	206,956	110,359	106,988	61,237	44,277	27,331	17,885	20,113	595,146
2005	215,771	118,390	109,371	61,433	45,307	27,849	18,590	21,066	617,777
2006	222,290	123,705	116,764	65,285	50,355	30,916	20,885	23,383	653,583
2007	207,785	125,585	121,574	68,876	52,875	31,929	21,891	25,899	656,414
2008	214,827	133,017	129,014	74,565	55,887	34,632	25,017	31,246	698,205
2009	200,625	127,976	125,026	70,888	49,986	31,673	23,405	30,666	660,245
2010	214,583	132,558	131,805	80,009	58,414	39,264	29,284	29,304	715,221
2011	219,899	140,072	135,413	91,659	66,582	45,572	35,384	37,659	772,240
2012	214,977	150,977	140,795	96,121	74,173	48,646	38,381	40,598	804,668
2013	236,625	146,744	135,705	96,183	77,325	53,592	42,918	43,804	832,896

Source: EMIS 2004/05–2013/14.

Table A3.3 (a) Promotion Rates—Girls (Standard 1 to Standard 7), 2004/05 to 2012/13

	Std 1	Std 2	Std 3	Std 4	Std 5	Std 6	Std 7
2004	51.3%	71.7%	62.7%	70.5%	67.6%	70.6%	68.3%
2005	52.2%	71.8%	63.1%	71.3%	67.9%	71.6%	69.5%
2006	51.7%	71.6%	62.7%	71.5%	68.4%	71.2%	68.8%
2007	62.0%	78.2%	68.3%	75.6%	72.4%	75.0%	73.9%
2008	60.3%	75.6%	65.6%	72.4%	71.5%	74.1%	70.7%
2009	62.2%	76.6%	68.4%	74.2%	72.5%	76.5%	72.6%
2010	62.2%	76.8%	69.1%	71.6%	71.4%	75.2%	68.1%
2011	60.6%	74.8%	69.1%	71.0%	69.6%	72.0%	64.7%
2012	64.8%	79.6%	72.8%	74.9%	72.4%	74.1%	67.3%

Source: EMIS 2004/05–2013/14.
Note: P1(2004) = Rate of promotion Std1 to Std2
P1(2004) = (Enrolment in Std2 in 2005–Repeaters in Std2 in 2005)/Enrolment in Std1 in 2004

Table A3.3 (b)   Promotion Rates—Boys (Standard 1 to Standard 7), 2004/05 to 2012/13

	Std 1	Std 2	Std 3	Std 4	Std 5	Std 6	Std 7
2004	53.0%	71.7%	62.5%	70.0%	68.4%	73.5%	77.0%
2005	52.2%	72.3%	61.9%	69.7%	67.9%	73.3%	78.3%
2006	52.0%	71.7%	62.0%	71.0%	68.8%	75.8%	79.5%
2007	63.1%	79.0%	66.9%	74.5%	73.3%	78.6%	83.4%
2008	59.6%	74.3%	64.4%	70.1%	70.7%	74.8%	79.9%
2009	63.2%	76.8%	68.0%	72.6%	72.9%	78.1%	79.0%
2010	60.9%	75.2%	68.3%	71.0%	71.2%	75.9%	75.8%
2011	62.2%	76.0%	68.3%	70.9%	71.0%	75.0%	75.1%
2012	64.6%	78.8%	72.7%	75.0%	73.3%	75.8%	75.7%

Source: EMIS 2004/05–2013/14.
Note: P1(2004) = Rate of promotion Std1 to Std2
P1(2004) = (Enrolment in Std2 in 2005–Repeaters in Std2 in 2005)/Enrolment in Std1 in 2004

Table A3.3 (c)   Promotion Rates—Standard 1 to Standard 7, 2004/05 to 2012/13

	Std 1	Std 2	Std 3	Std 4	Std 5	Std 6	Std 7
2004	52.1%	71.7%	68.9%	70.3%	68.0%	72.1%	72.9%
2005	52.2%	72.1%	69.0%	70.5%	67.9%	72.4%	74.1%
2006	51.9%	71.7%	69.1%	71.3%	68.6%	73.5%	74.3%
2007	62.6%	78.6%	74.9%	75.0%	72.9%	76.8%	78.8%
2008	59.9%	74.9%	71.2%	71.3%	71.1%	74.4%	75.4%
2009	62.7%	76.7%	74.7%	73.4%	72.7%	77.3%	75.8%
2010	61.6%	76.0%	76.1%	71.3%	71.3%	75.6%	72.0%
2011	61.4%	75.4%	76.2%	71.0%	70.3%	70.3%	69.9%
2012	64.7%	79.2%	80.0%	75.0%	72.9%	75.0%	71.6%

Source: EMIS 2004/05–2013/14.
Note: P1(2004) = Rate of promotion Std1 to Std2
P1(2004) = (Enrolment in Std2 in 2005–Repeaters in Std2 in 2005)/Enrolment in Std1 in 2004

Table A3.4 (a)   Repeater Rates—Girls (Standard 1 to Standard 8), 2004/05 to 2012/13

	Std 1	Std 2	Std 3	Std 4	Std 5	Std 6	Std 7	Std 8
2004	23.8%	21.2%	20.8%	16.1%	14.8%	12.1%	10.7%	13.7%
2005	25.4%	21.2%	22.3%	16.9%	16.1%	13.4%	11.7%	14.5%
2006	23.2%	21.4%	22.3%	17.1%	16.3%	13.1%	11.6%	15.3%
2007	24.8%	22.2%	23.3%	17.8%	16.7%	13.8%	12.9%	17.6%
2008	22.6%	19.1%	20.7%	15.8%	13.7%	11.3%	11.2%	15.9%
2009	24.1%	19.9%	21.1%	17.4%	15.7%	13.5%	12.8%	14.9%
2010	24.2%	20.5%	20.9%	17.7%	16.7%	14.7%	14.1%	17.7%
2011	22.8%	22.0%	20.9%	17.7%	17.0%	14.7%	14.5%	18.2%
2012	24.1%	19.8%	19.8%	17.4%	16.8%	15.3%	15.6%	19.1%

Source: EMIS 2004/05–2013/14.
Note: R1(2004) = Rate of repetition in Std1 (2004) = Repeaters in Std1 in 2005/Enrolment in Std1 in 2004

Table A3.4 (b) Repeater Rates—Boys (Standard 1 to Standard 8), 2004/05 to 2012/13

	Std 1	Std 2	Std 3	Std 4	Std 5	Std 6	Std 7	Std 8
2004	25.7%	20.5%	22.7%	17.0%	15.4%	12.5%	10.2%	14.8%
2005	26.1%	22.0%	22.9%	17.8%	16.8%	13.2%	11.3%	16.3%
2006	23.7%	22.4%	23.6%	18.4%	17.2%	13.7%	11.6%	17.2%
2007	26.0%	23.3%	25.0%	19.5%	17.2%	14.0%	12.5%	19.8%
2008	22.9%	19.5%	21.8%	16.8%	14.4%	11.8%	10.5%	16.8%
2009	25.0%	20.5%	21.3%	17.8%	16.7%	14.1%	12.9%	15.4%
2010	24.4%	20.7%	21.7%	18.6%	17.3%	15.5%	14.3%	19.5%
2011	23.7%	21.2%	22.3%	18.7%	17.8%	15.3%	14.7%	19.2%
2012	25.2%	21.0%	20.9%	17.9%	17.7%	15.5%	15.4%	19.9%

Source: EMIS 2004/05–2013/14.
Note: R1(2004) = Rate of repetition in Std1 (2004) = Repeaters in Std1 in 2005/Enrolment in Std1 in 2004

Table A3.4 (c) Repeater Rates, Standard 1 to Standard 8, 2004/05 to 2012/13

	Std 1	Std 2	Std 3	Std 4	Std 5	Std 6	Std 7	Std 8	Overall
2004	24.7%	20.9%	21.7%	16.6%	15.1%	12.3%	10.5%	14.3%	19.5%
2005	25.7%	21.6%	22.6%	17.3%	16.5%	13.3%	11.5%	15.5%	20.4%
2006	23.4%	21.9%	22.9%	17.7%	16.8%	13.4%	11.6%	16.4%	20.0%
2007	25.4%	22.7%	24.2%	18.7%	17.0%	13.9%	12.7%	18.8%	21.1%
2008	22.8%	19.3%	21.2%	16.3%	14.1%	11.5%	10.8%	16.4%	18.3%
2009	24.5%	20.2%	21.2%	17.6%	16.2%	13.8%	12.9%	15.1%	19.5%
2010	24.3%	20.6%	21.3%	18.2%	17.0%	15.1%	14.2%	18.6%	20.0%
2011	23.2%	21.6%	21.6%	18.2%	17.4%	15.0%	14.6%	18.7%	19.9%
2012	24.6%	20.4%	20.3%	17.7%	17.2%	15.4%	15.5%	19.5%	19.9%

Source: EMIS 2004/05–2013/14.
Note: R1(2004) = Rate of repetition in Std1 (2004) = Repeaters in Std1 in 2005/Enrolment in Std1 in 2004

Table A3.5 (a) Dropout Rates—Girls (Standard 1 to Standard 7), 2004/05 to 2012/13

	Std 1	Std 2	Std 3	Std 4	Std 5	Std 6	Std 7
2004	24.9%	7.1%	16.5%	13.3%	17.6%	17.4%	20.9%
2005	22.4%	7.0%	14.5%	11.8%	16.0%	14.9%	18.8%
2006	25.1%	7.0%	15.0%	11.4%	15.2%	15.7%	19.6%
2007	13.2%	0.0%	8.3%	6.6%	10.9%	11.2%	13.2%
2008	17.1%	5.3%	13.7%	11.8%	14.8%	14.7%	18.1%
2009	13.7%	3.5%	10.6%	8.4%	11.7%	10.0%	14.6%
2010	13.6%	2.8%	10.0%	10.6%	12.0%	10.1%	17.8%
2011	16.6%	3.1%	10.0%	11.3%	13.3%	13.3%	20.8%
2012	11.1%	0.6%	7.4%	7.7%	10.8%	10.6%	17.0%

Source: EMIS 2004/05–2013/14.
Note: D1(2004) = Rate of dropout from Std1 (2004)
D1(2004) = [Enrolment in Std1 in 2004–those promoted to Std2 in 2005–Repeaters in Std1 in 2004]/Enrolment in Std1 in 2004

Table A3.5 (b) Dropout Rates—Boys (Standard 1 to Standard 7), 2004/05 to 2012/13

	Std 1	Std 2	Std 3	Std 4	Std 5	Std 6	Std 7
2004	21.3%	7.7%	14.8%	13.1%	16.2%	14.0%	12.8%
2005	21.7%	5.7%	15.3%	12.5%	15.3%	13.5%	10.4%
2006	24.2%	5.9%	14.4%	10.6%	14.0%	10.5%	9.0%
2007	10.9%	-2.2%	8.1%	6.0%	9.5%	7.4%	4.1%
2008	17.5%	6.2%	13.8%	13.1%	14.9%	13.4%	9.5%
2009	11.7%	2.7%	10.6%	9.5%	10.4%	7.8%	8.1%
2010	14.6%	4.1%	9.9%	10.4%	11.4%	8.5%	9.9%
2011	14.1%	2.8%	9.4%	10.3%	11.3%	9.8%	10.2%
2012	10.2%	0.2%	6.4%	7.1%	9.0%	8.7%	8.9%

Source: EMIS 2004/05–2013/14.
Note: D1(2004) = Rate of dropout from Std1 (2004)
D1(2004) = [Enrolment in Std1 in 2004–those promoted to Std2 in 2005–Repeaters in Std1 in 2004]/Enrolment in Std1 in 2004

Table A3.5 (c) Dropout Rates, Standard 1 to Standard 7, 2004/05 to 2012/13

	Std 1	Std 2	Std 3	Std 4	Std 5	Std 6	Std 7
2004	23.2%	7.4%	9.4%	13.2%	16.9%	15.6%	16.6%
2005	22.1%	6.4%	8.4%	12.2%	15.6%	14.2%	14.4%
2006	24.7%	6.5%	8.0%	11.0%	14.6%	13.1%	14.1%
2007	12.1%	-1.3%	0.9%	6.3%	10.2%	9.3%	8.5%
2008	17.3%	5.7%	7.6%	12.4%	14.8%	14.0%	13.7%
2009	12.7%	3.1%	4.1%	9.0%	11.1%	8.9%	11.3%
2010	14.1%	3.5%	2.6%	10.5%	11.7%	9.3%	13.8%
2011	15.4%	2.9%	2.2%	10.8%	12.3%	14.7%	15.5%
2012	10.6%	0.4%	-0.4%	7.4%	9.9%	9.6%	12.9%

Source: EMIS 2004/05–2013/14.
Note: D1(2004) = Rate of dropout from Std1 (2004)
D1(2004) = [Enrolment in Std1 in 2004–those promoted to Std2 in 2005–Repeaters in Std1 in 2004]/Enrolment in Std1 in 2004

Table A3.6 Coefficient of Efficiency in Primary, 2004/05 to 2012/13

	Primary
2004	65.3%
2005	65.6%
2006	65.7%
2007	72.3%
2008	69.5%
2009	71.8%
2010	70.9%
2011	70.1%
2012	73.3%

Source: EMIS 2004/05–2013/14.
Note: Coefficient = Effective pupil-years/Total pupil-years in Std1 to Std8
Effective pupil-years = Σ(enrolment in Std1 × P1… enrolment in Std8 × P8)
Total pupil-years = Σ(enrolment in Std1… enrolment in Std8)

Table A4.1 Results from SACMEQ II (2002) and III (2007) on Teacher Performance

Teacher Performance in SACMEQ tests	SACMEQ II (2002)	SACMEQ III (2007)
Reading	**715.4 (5.79)**	**720.1 (5.69)**
Level 8: Critical Reading	58.40%	64.40%
Level 7: Analytical Reading	35.90%	29.90%
Level 6: Inferential Reading	3.30%	5.70%
Level 5: Interpretive Reading	0.90%	0%
Level 4: Reading for Meaning	1.40%	0%
Mathematics	**776.0 (8.66)**	**762.4 (8.45)**
Level 8: Abstract Problem Solving	29.40%	27.70%
Level 7: Concrete Problem Solving	10.50%	41.20%
Level 6: Mathematically Skilled	6.90%	16.30%
Level 5: Competent Numeracy	1.80%	12.20%
Level 4: Beginning Numeracy		2.70%

Source: SACMEQ II (2002) and SACMEQ III (2007).

Table A4.2 Average of Teaching Periods, 2011, 2012, and 2013

	2011	2012	2014
Average of periods taken per week	35.2	31	33.4
If one period is 35 min, total time in classroom periods in a week (hours)	20.5	18.1	19.5
Mean of hours per day	4.1	3.6	3.9
Number of teachers interviewed	1,572	1,081	241

Source: Open and Distance Learning Survey (ODL) for 2011 and 2012, QSDS 2014.

Table A4.3 Percent of Students with Textbooks (Classroom Observations), 2011 and 2012

	2011	2012
English textbooks		
Standard 3	28.4%	10.8%
Standard 4	37.3%	13.9%
Standard 5	22.8%	10.1%
Standard 6	17.3%	5.5%
Chichewa textbooks		
Standard 3	25.5%	9.7%
Standard 4	32.6%	8.9%
Standard 5	22.0%	9.7%
Standard 6	16.6%	4.9%
Mathematics textbooks		
Standard 3	27.9%	10.8%
Standard 4	36.3%	14.3%
Standard 5	26.5%	11.9%
Standard 6	18.4%	6.6%

table continues next page

Table A4.3 Percent of Students with Textbooks (Classroom Observations), 2011 and 2012
(continued)

	2011	2012
Exercise textbooks		
Standard 3	89.0%	96.5%
Standard 4	89.1%	97.3%
Standard 5	77.7%	97.5%
Standard 6	94.0%	98.4%

Source: Open and Distance Learning Survey (ODL) for 2011 and 2012, QSDS 2014.

APPENDIX B

Quality of Service Delivery Survey

QSD Survey 2014

The Quality of Service Delivery Survey (QSDS) 2014 was sponsored by the UK Department for International Development (DFID) and managed by the World Bank. Primary data were collected from a countrywide sample of 238 schools. Data collection was conducted from the 23rd of October to the 28th of November 2014.

Different information was collected under the QSD Survey, including information on head teachers, teachers, students and households. Additionally, some students in standard 5 and teachers were tested.

Number of schools	238
Schools with classroom observations (standard 5)	191
Schools surveyed with teachers	205
Teachers surveyed	241
Teachers tested	102
Students surveyed	2575
Students tested	744
Households with students	1664

School facility questionnaire	School	Contains school level information on infrastructure, school management etc. Information is collected from Head Teacher, and additional information is obtained from school records
Teacher questionnaire	Teacher	Contains information about teacher background, teacher training, and their attitudes and practices.
Classroom observation	Teacher/classroom	Contains information about classrooms, particularly the ambience, teaching learning materials, classroom organization etc.

table continues next page

Time on task	Classroom	Contains information on the main activities that were observed in every minute in a classroom and the nature of activities that were seen
Learner test results: standard 5	Student	Tests for students in standard 5
Student household	Household	Survey of households of students in standard 5 who took the test
Teacher test results	Teacher	Test results of teachers on the primary school curriculum

Bibliography

Drummond, Paulo, Vimal Thakur, and Shu Yu. 2004. "Africa Rising: Harnessing the Demographic Dividend." International Monetary Fund Working Paper, WP/14/143, Washington, DC.

Ministry of Education, Science and Technology. 2013. "Primary School Improvement Program, National Evaluation Report 2010/11 to 2012/13."

———. 2014. "Education Sector Implementation Plan II: Towards Quality Education—Empowering the Schools 2013–2018."

SACMEQ. 2010. "What Are the Levels and Trends in Reading and Mathematics Achievement?" SACMEQ Policy Issues Series, Number 2. http://www.sacmeq.org/sites/default/files/sacmeq/reports/sacmeq-iii/policy-issue-series/002-sacmeqpolicyissuesseries-pupilachievement.pdf.

UNICEF. 2012. "Monitoring Learning Achievement." (MLA) Draft Report UNICEF.

USAID. 2014. "Report for Study on Student Repetition and Attrition in Primary Education in Malawi." USAID. http://pdf.usaid.gov/pdf_docs/PA00K2HF.pdf.

World Bank. 2010. "Ethiopia Public Finance Review." Public Expenditure Review (PER), World Bank Group, Washington, DC.

———. 2013. "Malawi Public Expenditure Review." Public Expenditure Review (PER), World Bank Group, Washington, DC.

ECO-AUDIT

Environmental Benefits Statement

The World Bank Group is committed to reducing its environmental footprint. In support of this commitment, the Publishing and Knowledge Division leverages electronic publishing options and print-on-demand technology, which is located in regional hubs worldwide. Together, these initiatives enable print runs to be lowered and shipping distances decreased, resulting in reduced paper consumption, chemical use, greenhouse gas emissions, and waste.

The Publishing and Knowledge Division follows the recommended standards for paper use set by the Green Press Initiative. The majority of our books are printed on Forest Stewardship Council (FSC)–certified paper, with nearly all containing 50–100 percent recycled content. The recycled fiber in our book paper is either unbleached or bleached using totally chlorine free (TCF), processed chlorine free (PCF), or enhanced elemental chlorine free (EECF) processes.

More information about the Bank's environmental philosophy can be found at http://crinfo.worldbank.org/wbcrinfo/node/4.

CPSIA information can be obtained
at www.ICGtesting.com
Printed in the USA
LVHW100313261219
641613LV00007B/176/P